T0366853

Outlook
Pocket Guide

Walter Glenn

Beijing · Boston · Farnham · Sebastopol · Tokyo

Outlook Pocket Guide

by Walter Glenn

Copyright © 2003 O'Reilly Media, Inc. All rights reserved.
Printed in the United States of America.

Published by O'Reilly Media, Inc., 1005 Gravenstein Highway North,
Sebastopol, CA 95472.

O'Reilly & Associates books may be purchased for educational,
business, or sales promotional use. Online editions are also available
for most titles (*safari.oreilly.com*). For more information, contact our
corporate/institutional sales department: (800) 998-9938 or
corporate@oreilly.com.

Editor:	Nancy Kotary
Production Editor:	Genevieve d'Entremont
Cover Designer:	Emma Colby
Interior Designer:	David Futato

Printing History:

    March 2003:   First Edition.

978-0-596-00444-6
[LSI]

Contents

Part II. General Tasks

Part III. Mail Tasks

Part IV. Calendar Tasks

Part X. Outlook Resources

Outlook Pocket Guide

Introduction

This Pocket Guide is a quick-reference guide to the most recent versions of Microsoft Outlook—2000 and 2002. It is useful for both new and experienced users of Outlook and is put together in the following way:

- Part I provides an overview of the most important concepts for working in Outlook. It should leave you with a firm understanding of what Outlook does.

- Part II covers general tasks that apply no matter what specific function of Outlook you are using. These tasks are categorized by function for easy reference. While Parts II through VIII are designed primarily as a reference, you can learn a lot about Outlook from browsing through the tasks.

- Part III covers tasks related to setting up and using Outlook email.

- Part IV covers Outlook's calendar function.

- Part V covers Outlook's contact feature.

- Part VI covers Outlook's Task List.

- Part VII covers Outlook's note feature.

- Part VIII covers Outlook's journal.

- Part IX contains a number of reference tables so that you can quickly look up otherwise hard-to-find information.

- Part X lists several online resources, additional books, and Outlook add-in tools that may be useful to you.

Conventions Used in This Book

The following typographical conventions are used in this book:

Italic

> Indicates new terms, URLs, filenames, file extensions, directories, commands and options, and program names. For example, a path in the filesystem will appear as *C:\ Program Files\Microsoft Office*.

`Constant width`

> Shows the contents of files or the output from commands.

`Constant width bold`

> In examples and tables, shows commands or other text that should be typed literally by the user.

`Constant width italic`

> In examples and tables, shows text that should be replaced with user-supplied values.

Variable lists

> The variable lists throughout Parts II–VIII of this book present tasks as the answer to a "How do I…" question (e.g., "How do I find all messages from a particular person?").

Menus/Navigation

> Menus and their options are referred to in the text as File → New, Tools → Forms → Choose Form, and so on. Arrows are also used to signify a navigation path when using window options; for example, Tools → Options → Preferences → "Default reminder" means that you would open the Tools menu, select the Options command, switch to the Preferences tab, and select the "Default reminder" option on that tab.

Pathnames

Pathnames are used to show the location of a file or application in Windows Explorer. Folders are separated by a backward slash. For example, if you see something like, "…default location is *C:\Program Files\Microsoft Office*" in the text, that means the default location of the file being discussed is in the *Microsoft Office* subfolder of the *Program Files* folder.

Menu symbols

When looking at the menus for any application, you will see symbols associated with keyboard shortcuts for a particular command. For example, to print an item in Microsoft Outlook, you could go to the File menu and select Print (File → Print), or you could issue the keyboard shortcut, Ctrl-P.

TIP

Indicates a tip, suggestion, or general note.

WARNING

Indicates a warning or caution.

In Parts II–VIII, we've highlighted some of the especially cool and useful tips for you in these boxes. Even Outlook pros might learn a thing or two, or get a reminder about an old favorite trick.

02+

Used primarily in Parts II–VIII, this icon indicates that the features discussed are available only in Outlook 2002 and newer versions. Outlook 2000 does not support features marked with this icon.

PART I

Understanding Outlook

The first part of this book introduces the principal functions of Outlook. The intent of this part is to help new users hit the ground running and to provide experienced users with a keener understanding of why Outlook works (and sometimes doesn't work) the way it does.

Outlook provides six primary functions, all of which interact with one another. These functions include:

Email

> Set up any number of email accounts and manage them all from a single Inbox. Accounts can include Internet email accounts from an ISP or mailboxes on a company mail server, such as Microsoft Exchange Server. See Part III for tasks specific to this function.

Calendar

> Record appointments and meetings, view other people's calendars, and set up meetings automatically via email. See Part IV for calendar tasks.

Contacts

> Store information about people, such as addresses, phone numbers, email addresses, and much more. See Part V for contacts tasks.

Tasks

> Keep a running to-do list complete with due dates. See Part VI for tasks specific to this function.

Notes

Keep free-form text notes that don't fit anywhere else or temporarily store information here. See Part VII for notes tasks.

Journal

Automatically or manually record anything that happens in your life. See Part VIII for journal tasks.

Each of these major functions gets its own part in this book. You'll find tasks that apply to Outlook in general listed in Part II. Unlike Parts II–VIII, Part I (which you're reading now) is not really about specific tasks. Rather, it discusses the most important concepts of Outlook—the things that all Outlook users should understand. This part covers:

- The Outlook interface
- How Outlook stores information
- Folders and items
- Views
- Forms
- Shortcut menus
- Categories
- Address books
- Accounts
- Profiles

The Outlook Interface

Though many new elements have been added to Outlook over the years, the basic Outlook interface has not really changed too much. Figure 1-1 shows the Outlook interface with all optional views enabled and all the parts labeled. Your view of Outlook might look a little different, but probably just because you have some things (such as the Folder List) turned off. In the following discussion of the parts of the interface, you'll learn how to turn each part on or off.

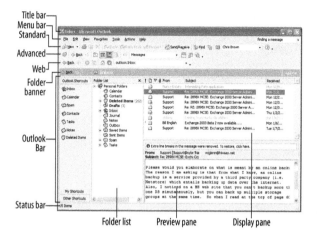

Figure 1-1. The Outlook interface

NOTE

The figures in this book are based on Outlook 2002; for the most part, you'll find that the interface is the same in Outlook 2000 and 2002. Any differences are indicated in the text.

The following list describes the important elements of the Outlook interface:

Title bar

The title bar shows the name of the folder you are currently working in. It also holds the Minimize, Maximize, and Close buttons for the Outlook window. Clicking the Outlook icon on the title bar reveals the control menu with additional window commands—you can get the same menu by right-clicking the Outlook taskbar button in Windows.

Menu bar

Menus hold all of the common commands available in Outlook. Commands on some of the menus (especially the Action menu) change depending on the type of folder selected (email, contacts, tasks, etc.). The menu bar (and other toolbars) are normally docked to the top of the window, but you can drag them to float anywhere on your screen (or just rearrange their docking order) using the handle at the far left of the bar. Outlook retains the positioning of menu and toolbars even after it is shut down.

A feature named adaptive menus is enabled by default, causing Outlook to show only the basic commands (as decided by Microsoft) and the most frequently used commands, unless you click an extra button to show the rest. You can turn off this feature using Tools → Customize → Options → Always Show Full Menus.

TIP

If you are learning Outlook, turn off adaptive menus. Being able to browse a full list of commands and find commands where you expect them is vital to the learning process. Even if you're experienced, consider turning the feature off and customizing your menus instead. See Part II for more on customizing.

Standard toolbar

Toolbars work much like menu bars and, in fact, can be customized to hold menus. The Standard toolbar holds buttons for common commands from the File, Edit, Tools, and Action menus. Figure 1-2 shows the commands you will *always* see on the Standard toolbar. Additional command buttons are added depending on the type of folder selected.

Figure 1-2. The Standard toolbar

1. The *New* button (also Ctrl-N) creates a new item based on the currently selected folder (e.g., a new email message opens when viewing an email folder). Click the down arrow to create a new item of another kind (including new folders and Outlook Bar shortcuts).

2. *Print* sends the currently selected item directly to the printer with no confirmation dialog. Use File → Print or Ctrl-P to open the Print dialog for more choices.

3. *Move to Folder* opens a submenu that lists recently accessed folders in Outlook. Select one from this list to move the currently selected item there, or choose Move to Folder to open a dialog with a full folder list. Ctrl-Shift-V also opens this dialog.

4. *Delete* moves the selected item to the Deleted Items folder. Press the Delete key for the same effect. Hold down Shift while using the Delete button or key to permanently delete the item.

5. *Find* (also Ctrl-E) opens a small Find bar directly above the Display pane, with fields for performing a quick search. The search defaults to the current folder. On the Find bar, use Options → Advanced Find for more sophisticated search tools. Without the Find bar open, use Tools → Advanced Find or Ctrl-Shift-F to open the same advanced search dialog.

6. *Organize* opens a new pane above the Display pane with commands for using folders, colors, and views to organize items and filter junk email. These tasks are covered in Part II.

---

7. *Address Book* opens the Windows Address Book, which is covered later in this part.

8. Type a name or part of a name in the *Find a Contact* box and press Enter to open a dialog displaying all contacts that match that name. Click the down arrow to the right of the box to view recent searches for contacts.

9. The *Help* button (also Help → Microsoft Outlook Help or F1) opens the Outlook help window.

Advanced toolbar

The Advanced toolbar is hidden by default. Turn it on using View → Toolbars → Advanced. The Advanced toolbar holds mostly navigational and view commands from the View menu. Figure 1-3 shows the buttons you will always see on the Advanced toolbar. Again, other commands are added when viewing certain folder types.

Figure 1-3. The Advanced toolbar

1. *Outlook Today* sends you to the Outlook Today page, a summary view of new messages and tasks.

2. *Back* and *Forward* work like browser commands, taking you back (or forward) to the item you were looking at previously—even if it was in a different folder. You can also press the Backspace key to go back.

3. *Up One Level* takes you up one level in the folder list.

4. *Folder List* and *Preview Pane* toggle the display of those panes in the Outlook window.

5. *Print Preview* (or File → Print Preview) opens a window that shows what the current item will look like

when printed. You can find more information about printing specific items throughout this book.

6. *Undo* (Edit → Undo or Ctrl-Z) undoes the last filing action (such as moving or deleting an item).

7. The *Current View* drop-down menu displays a list of views that you can use for the current folder. This list changes depending on the type of folder selected.

Web toolbar

The Web toolbar contains standard browser commands for controlling Outlook when it is used to view web pages. Commands on this menu do not change. This toolbar is hidden by default, but you can turn it on using View → Toolbars → Web.

TIP

A quick way to customize the buttons shown on any toolbar is to click the small down arrow at the far right, point to Add or Remove Buttons, and then choose the buttons you want displayed.

Folder banner

For the most part, the Folder banner is not very useful; unfortunately, you can't turn it off. It shows the name of the folder you are in (useful if you don't keep the folder list open or pay attention to the title bar), has back and forward commands that duplicate the function of those found on the Advanced toolbar, and has a few web-like fields and buttons that duplicate the functionality of those found on the Web toolbar. When viewing a calendar, it also shows the date range. You can also click the folder name to open the Folder List—a feature already provided by the Folder List button on the Advanced toolbar and the View → Folder List command.

In Outlook 2000, a similar version of this banner appears over the Display pane and Folder List (it does not extend over the Outlook Bar), but it does not hold the address box or web commands. It holds only the name of the folder, which you can click to open the Folder List.

Outlook Bar

The Outlook Bar is visible by default, but you can turn it on or off using View → Outlook Bar. The Outlook Bar is essentially a pretty holder for shortcuts to Outlook folders, individual Outlook items, web pages, or programs and files on your computer (or network). Left in its default setup, it's not nearly as useful as just leaving the Folder List open. However, you can customize the Outlook Bar to make it a pretty powerful tool. Check out Part II for more.

Folder List

The Folder List is not visible by default. You can turn it on using View → Folder List. You can also click the name of the folder in the folder banner to open the Folder List temporarily. A small pushpin icon appears in the upper-right corner of the list; click this to make the list stay open. The Folder List displays all Outlook folders in a familiar tree structure. While you can get around with other navigational commands, and a customized Outlook Bar can save you a lot of time, the Folder List is the final word on navigating Outlook. It shows the actual folder structure and every folder you have. Toggle it on or off using View → Folder List, the Folder List button on the Advanced toolbar, or by clicking the folder name on the Folder banner.

Display pane

> The Display pane shows all of the items in the selected
> folder. The view and function of the Display pane
> changes depending on what type of folder you view. For
> information on changing views and using the Display
> pane for a particular folder type, see the appropriate part
> of this book (e.g., see Part III for email folders).

Preview pane

> The Preview pane is hidden by default, but you can turn
> it on using View → Preview Pane. The Preview pane,
> available for most types of folders, shows the properties
> or contents of an item without having to open the item.
> For example, when an email message is selected (as in
> Figure 1-1), the Preview pane shows the basic email
> headers (From, To, Subject, and Cc) along with the mes-
> sage text.

Status bar

> Outlook's status bar really doesn't do much. When view-
> ing a folder, it shows the number of items in the folder.
> When viewing an email folder, it also shows how many
> unread messages are in the folder. When Outlook is
> sending and receiving mail, the status and any error
> alerts are shown on the righthand side.

How Outlook Stores Information

Even though the Folder List makes it appear that Outlook stores information in folders, it actually stores all information in a single nonrelational database file known as a Personal Store (a .pst file). The default Personal Store (created when you install Outlook) is named Personal Folders and is the top-level folder in the Folder List (refer to Figure 1-1). The actual .pst file created is named *Outlook.pst* and is found in one of two places:

- In Windows NT/2000/XP, it's found in *\Documents and Settings\<username>\Local Settings\Application Data\ Microsoft\Outlook*.

- In Windows 9x/Me, it's found in *\Windows Local Settings\Application Data\Microsoft\Outlook*.

NOTE

Outlook can also connect to the storage areas of other types of information services (such as Exchange Servers or IMAP-based mail servers) and view and manipulate the data there. In these cases, Outlook doesn't store the information; the stores are server-based. This section, and most of this book, concentrates on the way Outlook stores information locally—in Personal Stores.

You can create and access as many .pst files as you want. Just use File → New → Outlook Data File (File → New → Personal Folders File in Outlook 2000). Each Personal Store appears as a top-level folder in the Folder List hierarchy (see Figure 1-4). Some people use multiple .pst files for organizing different projects or for keeping business and personal items separate. The catch is that only one Personal Store can have a functioning Inbox to which incoming messages are delivered. By default, it is the store created when you install Outlook. For that reason, I've always found it more convenient to use a single set of Personal Folders and then use subfolders to organize my data.

Figure 1-4. Viewing multiple Personal Stores (.pst files)

NOTE

Even though only one Personal Store can have a functioning Inbox, you can choose which Personal Store should get incoming messages, but only in Outlook 2002. Go to Tools → E-Mail Accounts → View or change existing e-mail accounts → Deliver new e-mail to the following location.

One good use I've found for additional .pst files is archival. Outlook includes an AutoArchive feature that creates an additional .pst file on your system named *archive.pst* (in the same location as the *Outlook.pst* file). Settings found on Tools → Options → Other → AutoArchive let you adjust the name and location of this file and choose whether Outlook should automatically prompt you every once in a while to archive items older than a specified date. The idea is that removing old items from your main .pst file keeps you from having to look through so much old clutter and helps keep down the size of your main *.pst* file—improving performance and making for easier backups. This is a fairly nice feature if you don't mind indiscriminately archiving items based simply on their age.

I use a different method of archiving, in which I create a *.pst* that I use to archive finished projects. I just stick all emails, tasks, and other items having to do with that project into folders in a well-named *.pst*, back up that *.pst* somewhere, and then remove it from my Outlook view by right-clicking the top-level folder of that set of Personal Folders and choosing Close. Some people use a similar time-based archival method by creating a separate archive for each year (as in Figure 1-4). Any time you need to access old items, grab the backup and open the *.pst* in Outlook by choosing Open → Outlook Data File (Open → Personal Folders File in Outlook 2000).

Of course, the ability to open additional *.pst* files in Outlook also means that it is easy to take a copy of a *.pst* file from one computer and view it on another computer running Outlook.

Folders and Items

All information in a Personal Store is organized into folders, subfolders, and items—much the same way folders and files are organized in Windows. When you open the Folder List in Outlook, you can see that hierarchical folder structure. The biggest difference between Windows folders and Outlook folders is that Outlook folders are type-based. Each folder is designed to hold items of one of the following types:

- Email messages
- Contacts
- Calendar entries

- Tasks
- Notes
- Journal entries

You cannot put items of one type into a folder designed to hold items of a different type. The default set of Personal Folders holds a number of folders that must remain where they are—you cannot rename, move, or delete them. These folders include the following:

Inbox

> This is the location to which all email messages from all accounts are delivered. Outlook allows only one Inbox, no matter how many sets of Personal Folders you create.

Outbox

> This is a holding area for outgoing messages. When you click Send after creating a new message, the message is stored here. Messages in the Outbox are delivered according to specified events, such as when an Internet connection is established, at timed intervals, or when exiting the program. You can customize these events and even choose a different way of sending messages for different email accounts by going to Tools → Options → Mail Setup → Send/Receive. You can also send messages immediately without using the Outbox—use Tools → Options → Mail Setup → Send immediately when connected.

Sent Items

> By default, a copy of every message you send is stored in this folder. You can stop sent messages from being saved using Tools → Options → Preferences → E-mail Options → Save copies of messages in Sent Items folder.

Deleted Items

> When you delete an item, it goes to the Deleted Items folder, where it remains until you delete it again from this folder or use Deleted Items → Empty Deleted Items

Folder. If you take one of these actions, the item is permanently deleted. Until then, you can retrieve a deleted item by simply going to the Deleted Items folder, finding the item, and moving it somewhere else.

Drafts

Drafts are email messages that have not been sent. By default, any new message you create that is open for longer than three minutes is saved in this folder. An open message is then saved every three minutes. If you send the message, it is removed from the Drafts folder. In an open message window, choose File → Save As (or Ctrl-S) to save the message to the Drafts folder so you can finish it later. Open a message from the Drafts folder to finish it and send it. Use Tools → Options → Preferences → E-mail Options → Advanced E-mail Options to choose where drafts are saved and how often.

Calendar, Contacts, Tasks, Notes, and Journal

Unlike the previous five folders (which are all email folders), these are the default folders used to store items related to Outlook's other functions. You can find more information about how to use and control these folders in the pertinent parts of this book.

While you can't substantially alter these default folders, you can pretty much do what you want organizationally. Create a new folder using File → New → Folder. Give it a name, choose the type of item the folder will contain (task, mail, etc.), and then choose a place for it.

Even though a folder can hold only items of one type, you can put folders made for different types of items anywhere you want (e.g., a tasks folder can go inside an email folder). This provides a wonderful degree of organizational freedom. For example, you could create a master folder for a project and then create an email folder, task folder, notes folder, and calendar folder inside—each for storing and tracking items associated with the project (as in Figure 1-5). I always make the main folder for a project a notes folder so that I can store brief thoughts there and deal with them later.

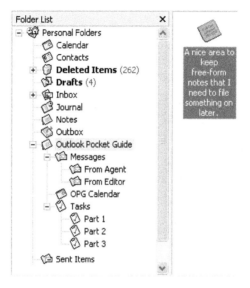

Figure 1-5. An example of organizational flexibility

Once your folder structure is set up to your liking, Outlook provides a number of ways to move items between folders:

- Simply drag an item to a different folder *that holds the same type of item* to move the item there. Hold Ctrl while dragging to copy the item instead. Drag with the right mouse button to pop up a small menu asking whether to move or copy.
- Select an item and choose Edit → Move to Folder (or press Ctrl-Shift-V). You can also right-click an item and

choose Move to Folder or use the Move to Folder button on the Standard toolbar.

- Click the Organize button on the Standard toolbar, make sure Using Folders is selected, and use the controls there to move the item selected in the Display pane.

TIP

You can drag items between different types of folders, but the effect is entirely different. Instead of moving the item, Outlook creates a new item of the target folder's type based on information from the item you drag. For example, dragging an email message to the contacts folder creates a new contact based on the sender of that message (and includes the text of the message in the note field of the contact). Dragging a contact to your Inbox creates a new email message to that contact. You can do this with pretty much every type of item.

Views

A view is simply how the information in a folder is displayed in the Display pane. Outlook provides a number of different predefined views that can be used to great effect in the various types of available folders. You can switch between different views to suit your style and even customize views extensively. While this sounds easy, you'd be surprised at how many people just use the default view for each folder and never go any farther.

There are two ways to change views for a current folder—choose View → Current View and then pick any of the views listed on that submenu, or use the Current View drop-down menu on the Advanced toolbar. If you don't see the Advanced toolbar, choose View → Toolbars → Advanced (or just right-click any toolbar and choose Advanced).

Outlook supports five basic types of views:

Table view
> This view displays items in a table format with each item on its own row and properties of that item in columns.

Card view
> This view displays each item in a format similar to an index card. Though most often used when displaying contacts, it can be useful with other items, too.

Day/Week/Month view
> This view displays items in a typical calendar format.

Timeline view
> This view displays items as icons on a horizontal timeline.

Icon view
> This view displays items as individual icons in the Display pane.

Of course, there are also many permutations of these five basic views—permutations that depend on things such as:

How fields are grouped
> For example, three of the built-in email views let you view messages grouped according to subject, sender, or to whom the message was sent. These are all table views—they're just grouped in different ways.

How fields are filtered
> Two of the predefined email views let you view messages according to a filter. The Unread Messages view shows only messages that have not been marked as read. The Last Seven Days view shows only messages whose received date falls within the last week.

And these are just a few examples. Experiment with all the different views available for each type of folder and you'll find that this ability to change your perspective on your data

---

is one of the more powerful features of Outlook. The built-in print styles used in Outlook (which you'll read about throughout this book) are also driven by views. You'll find a complete list of predefined views and print styles in Part IX.

NOTE

When the predefined views don't meet all your needs, you can modify them or even create your own. While there isn't room for this level of detail in a book like this, you can find pointers throughout the book and you can read an extensive treatment of the topic in *Outlook 2000 in a Nutshell*, by Tom Syroid and Bo Leuf (O'Reilly).

Forms

A form is the window you use to create or view an item. When you create a new email message and fill in the address, subject, and message body, you are using a form. When you open a contact and flip through the various tabs of information you can fill out about that person, that's also a form. And like many things in Outlook, forms are powerful, customizable, and sometimes complicated.

When you enter text in a form, most of the options you are used to using in other programs (such as Word) also apply. For example, you can undo an action (even perform multiple undos), double-click to select a word, use editing commands (cut, copy, and paste), and so on. Many of the fields you'll encounter on forms have formatting rules. For example, after you enter a phone number, Outlook will format it properly. After entering a name or address, Outlook may prompt you for clarification on which parts of those entries go where (e.g., which part of what you typed is a street address or a last name).

Every folder in Outlook has a form associated with it; this form is chosen when you decide what type of folder to create (or it's decided automatically for the predefined folders). For example, the Contact Form is associated with a contact folder. You can see the form associated with a folder by right-clicking the folder and choosing Properties; the "When posting to this folder, use" field shows the current form.

All of these forms are kept in a library named the Standard Forms Library. You can see the forms in this library using Tools → Forms → Choose Form or by using the drop-down list on a folder's Properties page. The Choose Form dialog that opens really just lets you choose a form and click Open to create a new item in the current folder, the same as if you had used the New command. You cannot choose a form type that the folder does not support.

Outlook comes with the following predefined forms:

Appointment and Meeting Request

Used for calendar folders. A meeting request is like a combination appointment and email message. An appointment is made in your calendar, and an email message is sent to whomever you address the message. The recipient of the message (if using Outlook) can then accept or reschedule the meeting.

Contact and Distribution List

Used in contact folders. A distribution list is a collection of contacts. When you send a message to a distribution list, the message goes to all the contacts in the list.

Journal Entry

Used only in journal folders. Many journal entries happen automatically (see Part VIII for more), but you can also create your own.

Message and Post

Used in email message folders. The Post Form is also used to post messages to an Exchange public folder.

TIP

Posting a message in an email folder (Inbox or anywhere else) is a great way to leave a note about a particular topic where you're sure to find it. I often post brief to-do items in my Inbox that don't require the full functionality of tasks.

Note

Used in note folders—a very simple text form.

Task and Task Request

Used in task folders. A task request is a special email message that asks the recipient to accept the task you define into their task folder (if they are using Outlook). Optionally, you can also add the same task to your own task folder and monitor its progress.

Standard Default

Used when the correct form for a folder cannot be found.

Shortcut Menus

If you have used Windows for any amount of time, you are likely familiar with shortcut menus: the contextual menus of commands you get when you right-click an item. Right-clicking also works in Outlook and is a real time-saver. Generally, right-clicking an element provides access to the same commands you would find on the regular menus for that element.

Here are a few examples of what right-clicking gets you in Outlook:

- An item's shortcut menu provides common commands such as printing, moving, deleting, and assigning categories. It also provides commands specific to the item— commands found on the Action menu or the Standard toolbar when an item of that type is selected. For example, right-clicking an email message lets you reply to or forward the message. Right-clicking a contact lets you create a new message, appointment, or task for the contact.

- A folder's shortcut menu provides the same commands found on the File → Folder menu and lets you do things like move, copy, delete, and rename the folder; add it to the Outlook Bar; or open the folder in a new window.

The same shortcut menu opens when you click a folder's Folder banner.

- Right-clicking anywhere on the toolbars or menu bar lets you turn toolbars on or off.

- Right-clicking a shortcut on the Outlook Bar lets you rename or remove the shortcut, as well as perform a few commands on the folder or item it targets.

- Right-clicking anywhere on the Outlook Bar (except on a shortcut) lets you change the Outlook Bar to small or large icons, as well as add, remove, or rename groups.

- Right-clicking the column header at the top of the Display pane (when viewing a table view) provides commands for sorting, grouping, and choosing fields, as well as for adjusting the view.

Using Categories

A category is a keyword that you assign to any type of item in order to associate the item with a group, project, or concept. You can then use categories to perform searches and group or filter views. For example, two predefined categories are Business and Personal. After assigning these categories to items, you can perform a search to find all business-related items scattered across all of the folders in Outlook. Or, you can customize a view so that only business items (or only personal items) are displayed in your Inbox. To make categories even more powerful, you can assign any item to multiple categories. Imagine being able to filter a view to show only contacts assigned to the categories "business" and "holiday cards."

To assign a category to an item, right-click the item and choose Categories (or select it and choose Edit → Categories). Select the categories you want and click OK (see

Figure 1-6). Some forms used to create items (such as the Contacts form) let you create categories while creating the items; others (such as the Message form) do not.

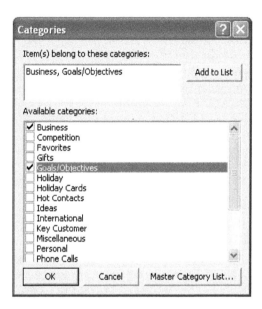

Figure 1-6. Assigning categories to items

You can type a new category directly into the box at the top of the Categories dialog and click Add to List, but this will only add the category for the current item and will not make that category usable for all items. I have never figured out how this option is useful.

To create and modify categories so that they are available for all items, you must use the Master Category List (Edit → Categories → Master Category List). This simple dialog lets you add and remove categories or reset the list to its default.

WARNING

Resetting the Master Category List returns any categories you have deleted and deletes any categories you have created. Items that have deleted categories assigned to them will still have those categories assigned to them; the categories will just no longer be available on the master list.

Address Books

Address books contribute a lot of confusion because, on many computers, there are more than one. Actually, there are three types of address books you might see when you use the Address Book tool in Outlook (Tools → Address Book, Ctrl-Shift-B, or press the To button on any message form).

Global Address List

This is used only if you are using Outlook to connect to an Exchange server, a network mail server used on many company networks. The Global Address List (GAL) is the list of all recipients in the Exchange organization, including mailboxes, distribution lists, and public folders.

Offline Address Book

This is also used only when connected to an Exchange server. The Offline Address Book (OAB) contains selected recipients from a GAL that are copied to your computer so that you can still address messages to them when you are not actually connected to the network.

Outlook Address Book

This is the primary address book you will use in Outlook. It is essentially a container used for viewing certain recipients from contact folders—specifically, those recipients that have either an email address or a fax number entered for them. By default, any new contact folder you create (and also the predefined Contacts folder) is included in the Outlook Address Book. You can change this by right-clicking a folder and choosing Properties → Outlook Address Book → Show this folder as an E-mail Address Book.

The Address Book provides a simple way to find recipients and address email messages, but it is not the only way. Here are just some of the ways you can get an email to the right person:

- Open the Address Book (Tools → Address Book or Ctrl-Shift-B) and pick a recipient from one of the available lists.

- Create a new email message. Click the To (or Cc or Bcc) button and use the dialog to find the right address list and then the right recipient.

- Create a new email message. In the To (or Cc or Bcc) field, start typing the name of the recipient (for example, "John"). In Outlook 2002, a drop-down menu appears with choices based on what you have typed. In Outlook 2000, a best guess is made based on what you typed, and this guess is underlined in red. Right-click it to open a menu with alternate choices from your address book. You can also just type in a full email address.

- Right-click any contact and choose New Message to Contact.

Accounts

Outlook is a messaging client that you can set up to access any number of messaging servers. Servers process, deliver, and store mail until a client connects with them and tells the server what to do with the mail. All email messages come to you via a server, whether that is an Exchange (or other) server on your company's local network, an email server run by your ISP, or a web-based email server like Microsoft Hotmail.

An email account is a collection of settings that tells Outlook how to contact and interact with a particular server. When you run Outlook for the first time, a wizard walks you through setting up your first email account. To add and manage accounts later, use Tools → E-Mail Accounts in Outlook 2002 and Tools → Accounts in Outlook 2000. (Specific account tasks are covered in Part III.)

Outlook supports accounts for the following types of servers:

Microsoft Exchange Server
> Exchange Server is Microsoft's network email server. If an Exchange server is running on your network, your administrator will either configure the account for you or provide the necessary information for you to configure the account.

POP3 (Post Office Protocol)
> POP3 is a popular protocol used for retrieving messages from an Internet mail server. If you connect to an ISP to access the Internet and get mail, it is very likely you are using POP3. When Outlook connects to a POP3 server, Outlook downloads all of the messages on the server to your computer and then optionally deletes those messages from the server. This means that all messages are stored on your computer. To configure a POP3 account, you will need information such as the email address, the exact name or address of the servers that receive incoming and send outgoing messages, and your username and password.

IMAP (Internet Message Access Protocol)
> IMAP is less popular than POP3, but quite useful if you regularly check your email from different computers. Unlike POP3 (which downloads messages from the server), IMAP stores messages on the server and lets you create folders on the server for organizational purposes. Messages are left on the server, and clients like Outlook only read and manage them.

HTTP (Hypertext Transfer Protocol)

HTTP is the protocol used to transfer information between web browsers and servers; it is increasingly being used for web-based email services like Hotmail and Yahoo! mail. Outlook 2002 supports web-based email servers. Outlook 2000 does not.

Additional server types

When you create a new account, you'll see this option. It is used to provide support for third-party email servers that might be on a company network and requires the installation of appropriate software on your computer so Outlook can interact with those servers.

Profiles

A profile is a collection of settings defining how Outlook is set up for a particular user. Profiles are intended to allow more than one person to use Outlook on the same computer or to allow users on a network to work from any computer and still access their settings. Profiles contain the following information:

- Customizations made in the Outlook interface
- Address Books
- Information about the configured email accounts
- The location of any Personal Stores (*.pst* files) associated with the account

---

NOTE

Profiles also allow users on a network to roam, meaning that they can log on from different computers on the network and still access their Outlook settings. I won't cover that topic in this book because a network administrator must set up this feature.

Most people will need only one profile and, if you install Outlook yourself and only use it yourself, you may never have to deal with profiles at all. If more than one person uses Outlook to get messages, profiles are easy enough to set up. The trick is that profiles are not managed within the Outlook interface. Instead, open the Windows Control Panel and then open the Mail tool to create and manage profiles.

PART II

General Tasks

This section of the book is designed to give you quick answers about how to perform basic tasks that apply regardless of what Outlook function you are using—email, calendar, and so on. Tasks are divided into the following categories:

- Finding your stuff
- Organizing your stuff
- Using the Outlook Bar
- Configuring other options
- Changing views
- Customizing menus and toolbars

Within these categories, tasks are presented as answers to "How do I..." questions (e.g., "How do I find items that belong to certain categories?"), followed by concise instructions for completing the task.

Finding Your Stuff

Search the current folder for items containing specific text?

Tools → Find, Ctrl-E, or click Find on the Standard toolbar. This opens a small search bar at the top of the display pane (Figure 2-1). Type the search text in the Look for box, click Search In to choose a different folder, then click Find Now. Results are displayed in the Display pane, so you won't be able to see items from the current folder until you close the Find bar (use the close button at the far right).

!	□	♥	Ø	From	Subject	Received	Size	▲
!	◻			Bill English	Exchange 2003 Beta 2 now available......	Mon 1/6/2...	4 KB	
				Neil J. Salkind	RE: Word Power Tools contract for O'Reilly	Tue 1/7/2...	4 KB	
				Neil J. Salkind	RE: Word Power Tools contract for O'Reilly	Tue 1/7/2...	4 KB	
			Ø	Stacey Barone	Walter Glenn - O'Reilly - Word Power Tools - Contr...	Wed 1/8/...	48 KB	
				Neil J. Salkind	FW: Software Forensics: Case Studies and Gener...	Thu 1/9/2...	18 KB	
			Ø	Stacey Barone	FW: Walter Glenn - O'Reilly - Word Power Tools - ...	Mon 1/13/...	49 KB	
				Neil J. Salkind	FW: Walter Glenn	Wed 1/15...	18 KB	
				Neil J. Salkind	RE: Walter Glenn	Wed 1/15...	21 KB	
				Stacey Barone	RE: Walter Glenn - O'Reilly - Word Power Tools - C...	Wed 1/15...	11 KB	
				Neil J. Salkind	RE: Glenn, English, Stanek - Exchange	Thu 1/16/...	7 KB	
			Ø	Criss Ashwell	Nothing To Do In Huntsville?	Fri 1/17/2...	13...	
				Jeff Koch (MSPRESS)	FW: Glenn, English, Stanek - Exchange	Fri 1/17/2...	8 KB	▼

Figure 2-1. Performing a simple find

Perform an advanced find?

Tools → Options → Advanced Find or Ctrl-Shift-F to open the Advanced Find dialog (Figure 2-2). You can also right-click a folder and choose Advanced Find to open the dialog with a specific folder selected. Use the Look For box to choose the Outlook item type you want to search for. Click Browse to change the search folder. By default, all subfolders are included in the search, so choosing the Personal Folders folder searches an entire *.pst* file. For a text search, enter the search text in the "Search for the word(s)" box and use the In drop-down list to choose the fields to search. Click Find Now to start searching. Search results appear in a pane below the search options.

Find all messages from or to a particular contact or contacts?

Tools → Advanced Find or Ctrl-Shift-F. Enter the contact in the From or Sent To field or click the From button to select from your address book.

Find all items in a certain date range?

Tools → Advanced Find or Ctrl-Shift-F. Use the Time fields.

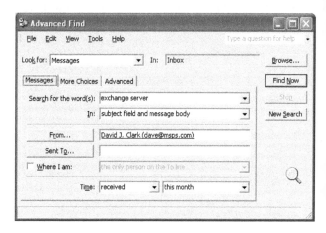

Figure 2-2. Advanced Find provides many options for searching folders

Find items that belong to certain categories?
Tools → Advanced Find or Ctrl-Shift-F. Use More Choices → Categories.

Search for items based on size?
Tools → Advanced Find or Ctrl-Shift-F. Use the Size fields.

Search for items based on importance?
Tools → Advanced Find or Ctrl-Shift-F. Use the "Whose importance is" option.

Find all read or unread items?
Tools → Advanced Find or Ctrl-Shift-F. Use the "Only items that are" option.

Find all items with or without attachments?
Tools → Advanced Find or Ctrl-Shift-F. Use the "Only items with" option.

Search for items based on multiple criteria?
> Tools → Advanced Find → Advanced. Use the Field button to select a criteria, fill in the options, and click Add to List. Click Find Now when your conditions are set.

Save an advanced search?
> Perform the advanced search and use File → Save Search.

Open a saved advanced search?
> Tools → Advanced Find → Open Search.

NOTE

There are many more options for performing advanced searches than can be covered here. For example, the choices change depending on the type of Outlook item for which you are searching. Explore the options under Tools → Advanced Find to find out what you can do.

Organizing Your Stuff

Switch to the Outlook Today page?
> On the Outlook Bar, click Outlook today.

> In the Folder List, select Personal Folders (Outlook 2002) or Outlook Today (Outlook 2000).

Customize the appearance of Outlook Today?
> Switch to the Outlook Today page and click "Customize Outlook Today..." at the upper-right of the date display bar. Choose which folders to display, how many calendar days to show, how tasks are configured, and a style.

Open a folder in a new window?
> In the Folder List or Outlook Bar, right-click the folder and choose Open in New Window.

Create a folder?
> Right-click the folder in the Folder List or Outlook Bar, or right-click the folder name in the Folder banner and use Open in New Window.

Copy a folder?

Select the folder and use File → Folder → Copy, or right-click the folder and choose Copy. In the dialog that opens, select the location to create the copy.

Hold Ctrl while dragging the folder to a new location in the Folder List.

Move a folder?

Select the folder and use File → Folder → Move, or right-click the folder and choose Move. In the dialog that opens, select the location to create the copy.

Drag the folder to a new location in the Folder List.

Rename a folder?

Right-click the folder and choose Properties. Type a new name into the top field on the General tab. Note that you cannot rename any of the default folders.

In the Folder List, click the folder name twice with a pause between clicks. Type a new name once the editing field appears on the name of the folder.

Delete a folder?

Select the folder and use Edit → Delete or press the Delete key.

Drag the folder to the Deleted Items folder.

Right-click the folder and choose Delete "folder_name".

Find out the size of a folder?

Right-click the folder and choose Properties → Folder Size.

Set a home page for a folder?

Right-click the folder and choose Properties → Home Page.

Configure AutoArchive settings specific to a folder?

Right-click the folder and choose Properties → Autoarchive. Use this tab to override the default AutoArchive settings for Outlook (discussed later in this part).

Create a new data file (.pst file)?
> File → New → Outlook Data File.

Move or copy items to a different .pst file?
> Make sure both *.pst* files are open and are displayed in the Folder List. Drag items to a folder in the other file.

Open an additional .pst file?
> File → Open → Outlook Data File.

Reduce the size of a .pst file?
> File → Data File Management. Select a data file and click Settings. Click Compact Now.

Assign a password to a .pst file?
> File → Data File Management. Select a data file and click Settings → Change Password.

WARNING

If you assign a password to a data file and then forget the password, there is no way built in to Outlook to recover the data from the file. You might be able to find a password-cracking program that will work. Try the software available at *http://www.crak.com* to start.

Import items from a .pst file?
> File → Import and Export. Choose "Import from another program or file," click Next, and choose Personal Folder File (*.pst*) from the list. Show the wizard where to find the file, and it will present you with a list of items it can import.

Export items to a .pst file?
> File → Import and Export. Choose Export to a File, click Next, and choose Personal Folder File (*.pst*) from the list. Choose what items to export and show Outlook where to save the export file.

Import and export other file types?
> File → Import and Export.

Using the Outlook Bar

Show or hide the Outlook Bar?
   View → Outlook Bar.

Switch groups on the Outlook Bar?
   Groups are the horizontal buttons on the Outlook Bar used to group icons. Click one to switch to that group.

Create a shortcut on the Outlook Bar?
   By default, Outlook offers to create a shortcut on the Outlook Bar for any new folder you create.

   Right-click anywhere in the group where you want to create the shortcut and choose Outlook Bar shortcut. The dialog that opens lets you create a shortcut to any Outlook folder, Outlook item, folder or document in Windows, or web page.

   You can also drag a folder to the Outlook Bar from the Folder List to quickly create a shortcut.

Delete a shortcut from the Outlook Bar?
   Right-click the shortcut and choose Remove from Outlook Bar.

Move a shortcut to another location on the Outlook Bar?
   Drag the shortcut over the name bar of the group to which you want to move it. The group will "spring" open, and you can drop the shortcut where you want it.

Change between large and small icons for an Outlook Bar group?
   Right-click anywhere in the group and choose Large Icons or Small Icons.

Add a new group to the Outlook Bar?

Right-click the Outlook Bar and choose Add New Group. The group appears at the bottom of the Outlook Bar. Name it and start moving shortcuts to it. This feature represents the real power of the Outlook Bar. A customized Outlook Bar is shown in Figure 2-3.

Figure 2-3. The Outlook Bar

Remove a group from the Outlook Bar?
   Right-click the group and choose Remove Group. You will lose all shortcuts in the group when you do this.

Rename a group on the Outlook Bar?
   Right-click the group and choose Rename Group.

Configuring Other Options

Empty the Deleted Items folder every time I exit Outlook?

Tools → Options → Other → Empty the Deleted Items folder upon exiting.

02+ *Make Outlook the default program in Windows for email, calendar, and contacts?*

The first time you run Outlook, it offers to make itself the default program for these actions. If you choose not to, you can do so later using Tools → Options → Other → "Make Outlook the default program for E-Mail, Contacts, and Calendar."

Specify how often the AutoArchive feature runs?

Tools → Options → Other → AutoArchive → Run AutoArchive every *xx* days.

Have Outlook ask me before running AutoArchive?

Tools → Options → Other → AutoArchive → Prompt before AutoArchive runs.

Delete expired items when AutoArchive runs?

Tools → Options → Other → AutoArchive → Delete expired items (email folders only).

Specify whether items are archived or deleted during AutoArchive?

In Outlook 2002, Tools → Options → Other → AutoArchive → Archive or delete old items. Choose whether to permanently delete items or move them to a *.pst* file.

02+ *Specify how old items must be before they are handled by AutoArchive?*

Tools → Options → Other → AutoArchive → Clean out items older than.

02+ *Enable Instant Messaging in Outlook?*

Tools → Options → Other → Enable Instant Messaging in Microsoft Outlook.

Changing Views

Change a view for a folder?

> View → Current View or use the Current View drop-down list on the Advanced toolbar.

Set the default view for a folder?

> Right-click the folder and choose Properties → Administration. Choose a view from the "Initial view on folder" drop-down list.

Sort a table view using a particular column?

> Click the column to sort the table by that column. Click the column again to reverse the sort order. A small triangle at the right side of the column label indicates ascending or descending sort order.

Create a custom sort for a view?

> View → Current View → Customize Current View → Sort. Use the "Sort items by" box to choose a sort field and choose ascending or descending order. Use the additional boxes to create a nested sort order (e.g., sort by subject, then by sender, then by date).

Remove a custom sort order?

> View → Current View → Customize Current View → Sort → Clear All.

Group items in a view using the Group By box?

> View → Current View → Customize Current View → Group By. As with sorting, you can set up a nested set of sorts by choosing fields and sort orders (Figure 2-4).
>
> You can open a different kind of grouping view by right-clicking a column header and choosing Group By. This opens a Group By pane over the Display pane. It works like the Group By dialog shown in Figure 2-4, except you drag fields to it to set up the grouping (Figure 2-5).

Figure 2-4. Setting up a grouping

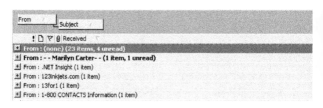

Figure 2-5. A different way to group items

Remove custom groupings?

> View → Current View → Customize Current View → Group By → Clear All.

Apply a filter to a view?

View → Current View → Customize Current View → Filter. Use the dialog to set options for the items you want to show (or not show). When you click OK, the filter is applied and only the items that meet the criteria are displayed.

Remove a filter?

View → Current View → Customize Current View → Filter → Clear All.

Add fields or columns to a table view?

View → Current View → Customize Current View → Fields. Select the fields from the Available fields list and click Add to add them to the view.

 You can also right-click the column header in any table view and select Field Chooser. Drag any field from the chooser to the column in the view to place it there.

Move a column to a new location?

Drag the column to a spot between two other columns.

Remove a column?

View → Current View → Customize Current View → Fields. Select the fields from the "Show these fields in this order" list and click Remove to remove them from the view.

You can also drag a column off the column header while in the view. A large X is placed over the icon to show that you are removing it.

Change the format of a column?

View → Current View → Format Columns, or right-click a column header and choose Format Columns. Use the Format field to change a column's format.

Change the label of a column heading?

View → Current View → Format Columns → Label. Whatever you type will appear in the column header.

Assign a specific width to a column?
> View → Current View → Format Columns → Width.

Align the contents in a column?
> View → Current View → Format Columns → Alignment.

Change other settings for a view?
> View → Current View → Customize Current View → Other Settings, or right-click a blank area in any view and choose Other Settings. Most of the details of these settings are explained throughout this book in the parts appropriate to the type of folder you are viewing.

Create a new view from scratch?
> View → Current View → Define Views → New. Name the view, choose a type, and click OK. You can then customize the view using any of the methods discussed so far.

Create a view based on another view?
> View → Current View → Define Views. Select an existing view and click Copy.

Change the name of a view?
> View → Current View → Define Views. Select a view and click Rename.

Delete a custom view?
> View → Current View → Define Views. Select a custom view and click Delete.

Reset a default view?
> View → Current View → Define Views. Select a default view and click Reset.

NOTE

The Delete and Reset buttons alternate depending on whether you have selected a custom or default view. You can delete custom views, but you cannot reset them. You can reset default views, but you cannot delete them.

Customizing Menus and Toolbars

Have Outlook show the full menus instead of adaptive menus?
Tools → Customize → Options → Always show full menus.

Use larger icons on toolbars?
Tools → Customize → Options → Large icons.

Turn off or on the pop-up balloon tips showing the names of toolbar buttons?
Tools → Customize → Options → Show Screen Tips on toolbars.

Have Outlook show shortcut keys for toolbar buttons in pop-up balloon tips?
Tools → Customize → Options → Show Shortcut Keys in ScreenTips.

Create a new toolbar that I can fill with buttons and menus?
Tools → Customize → Toolbars → New.

Rename a toolbar that I have created?
Tools → Customize → Toolbars. Select a toolbar and click Rename.

Restore a toolbar to its default settings?
Tools → Customize → Toolbars. Select a toolbar and click Reset.

Add a command to a toolbar or menu?
Tools → Customize → Commands. Select a category and then a command from that category. Click Description to view a pop-up explanation of the command. Drag the command to any toolbar or menu.

Remove a command from a toolbar or menu?
Tools → Customize. Drag the command from the menu and, when the icon displays an X, drop the command to remove it.

Without opening the Customize dialog, hold down the Alt key while dragging any command away from the toolbar.

Change the name of a menu command or toolbar button?
Tools → Customize. Right-click a command or button and change the value of the Name box on the shortcut menu. For many commands, an ampersand (&) indicates which letter in the command is underlined. Pressing the key for an underlined letter activates the command when using the Alt key to browse menus.

Change the icon used for a command or toolbar button?
Tools → Customize. Right-click a command or button and choose Change Button Image.

Change how text is displayed for a command or toolbar button?
Tools → Customize. Right-click a command or button and choose Default Style, Text Only (Always), Text Only (In Menus), or Image and Text.

Insert a dividing line between buttons on a toolbar or commands on a menu?
Tools → Customize. Right-click a command or button that will be to the right of (or below) the dividing line and choose Begin a Group.

PART III

Mail Tasks

This part provides quick answers about the most important of Outlook's major functions—email. Tasks are divided into the following eight categories:

- Setting up email accounts
- Creating and using messages
- Viewing messages
- Attaching items to messages
- Using signatures and stationery
- Managing messages
- Using rules
- Taming junk email

Within these categories, tasks are presented as answers to "How do I..." questions (e.g., "How do I include a vCard with my signature?"), followed by concise instructions for completing the task.

Setting Up Email Accounts

Add an email account?

The first time you start Outlook, a wizard walks you through setting up a default account.

To set up additional accounts in Outlook 2002, use Tools → E-Mail Accounts → Add a new e-mail account → Next to start this same wizard.

For Outlook 2000, use Tools → Accounts → Add → Mail.

Table 3-1 lists the information you'll need for each account type before you start the wizard.

Table 3-1. Email account information

Account type	Required info	Optional info	Notes
Exchange Server	Name or address of Exchange Server Username or mailbox name	Other settings provided by the network administrator	To add an Exchange account, you must close Outlook and use the Mail applet in the Windows Control Panel instead. You may or may not need a password, depending on network setup.
POP3 or IMAP	Username Password Email address Name or address of incoming and outgoing mail servers	Username and password for outgoing mail server, if required	
HTTP	Username Password Email address URL (web address) of server if not using Hotmail or MSN		
Additional server types	Information provided by the system administrator		

Remove an email account?

In Outlook 2002, Tools → E-mail Accounts → View or change existing e-mail accounts → Next. Choose an account from the list and click Remove.

In Outlook 2000, Tools → Accounts. Select the account and click Remove.

Change settings for an existing email account?

In Outlook 2002, Tools → E-mail Accounts → View or change existing e-mail accounts → Next. Select the account and click Change.

In Outlook 2000, Tools → Accounts. Select the account and click Properties.

Change the default email account?

In Outlook 2002, Tools → E-mail Accounts → View or change existing e-mail accounts → Next. Select the account and click Set as Default. The default account is used to create and send new messages, unless an alternate account is specified when the message is created.

In Outlook 2000, Tools → Accounts. Select the account and click Set as Default.

Change the order in which Outlook checks for mail on email accounts?

In Outlook 2002, Tools → E-mail Accounts → View or change existing e-mail accounts → Next. Select an account and use the Move Up and Move Down buttons to set the order.

In Outlook 2000, Tools → Accounts → Set Order. Select an account and use the Move Up and Move Down buttons to set the order.

Have replies to my messages sent to a different address than the one used to send the message?

In Outlook 2002, Tools → E-mail Accounts → View or change existing e-mail accounts → Next. Select the account, click Change → More Settings, and enter an address into the Reply E-mail field.

In Outlook 2000, Tools → Accounts. Select the account, click Properties, and enter an address into the Reply address field.

Change the name of an email account?

In Outlook 2002, Tools → E-mail Accounts → View or change existing e-mail accounts → Next. Select the account, click Change → More Settings, and enter the new name into the Mail Account field at the top of the General tab.

In Outlook 2000, Tools → Accounts. Select the account, click Properties, and enter the name into the Mail Account field at the top of the General tab.

Change the username or password for an email account?

In Outlook 2002, Tools → E-mail Accounts → View or change existing e-mail accounts → Next. Select the account, click Change, and enter the new information into the User Name and Password fields. Click Remember password so you don't have to type it in each time.

In Outlook 2000, Tools → Accounts. Select the account, click Properties → Servers, and enter the new information into the Account Name and Password fields. Click Remember password so you don't have to type it in each time.

Change the .pst file that contains the active Inbox for POP3 email accounts?

In Outlook 2002, Tools → E-mail Accounts → View or change existing e-mail accounts → Next → Deliver new e-mail to the following location.

In Outlook 2000, right-click the root folder of the Personal Folders file in which you want to receive messages and choose Properties → Deliver POP mail to this personal folders file. (See Part I for more on Personal Folders.)

NOTE

Why can you change only the delivery location for POP3 accounts? Because they are the only accounts that download messages and store them locally. Other account types leave messages on a mail server, and Outlook just accesses them. See Part I for more on this.

Change the names or addresses of the mail servers used for an account?

In Outlook 2002, Tools → E-mail Accounts → View or change existing e-mail accounts → Next. Select the account, click Change, and enter the information into the "Incoming mail server" and "Outgoing mail server" fields.

In Outlook 2000, Tools → Accounts. Select the account, click Properties → Servers, and enter the information into the "Incoming mail server" and "Outgoing mail server" fields.

Configure logon information if an outgoing mail server requires it?

In Outlook 2002, Tools → E-mail Accounts → View or change existing e-mail accounts → Next. Select the account and click Change → More Settings → Outgoing Server → "My outgoing server (SMTP) requires authentication." Enter the details.

In Outlook 2000, Tools → Accounts. Select the account and click Properties → Servers → My server requires authentication → Settings. Enter the details.

Test an account's settings to make sure I can send and receive messages?

In Outlook 2002, Tools → E-mail Accounts → View or change existing e-mail accounts → Next. Select an account, click Change, and then click Test Account Settings. Outlook sends a test message to your own address and checks to see if you receive it.

Outlook 2000 does not provide a one-click method for testing settings. Instead, configure the account, go back to Outlook, and try a Send/Receive. If you don't get any errors, try sending yourself an email.

Change the organization listed for an account?

In Outlook 2002, Tools → E-mail Accounts → View or change existing e-mail accounts → Next. Select an account, click Change → More Settings, and enter the name into the Organization field.

In Outlook 2000, Tools → Accounts. Select an account, click Properties, and enter the name into the Organization field.

Specify the connection method used for an account?

In Outlook 2002, Tools → E-mail Accounts → View or change existing e-mail accounts → Next. Select an account and use Change → More Settings → Connection.

In Outlook 2000, Tools → Accounts. Select an account and use Properties → Connection.

Change the TCP port numbers used to send and receive messages for a specific account?

In Outlook 2002, Tools → E-mail Accounts → View or change existing e-mail accounts → Next. Select an account, click Change → More Settings → Advanced, and enter the information into the "Incoming server" and "Outgoing server" fields.

In Outlook 2000, Tools → Accounts. Select an account, click Properties → Advanced, and enter the information into the "Incoming server" and "Outgoing server" fields.

WARNING

A port is like a channel your networking protocol uses to send and receive messages. The default values are set to standards that are used by mail servers across the world. Do not change the values unless you are sure your mail servers are set to use different ports.

Have Outlook leave a copy of messages on a POP3 server instead of deleting them?

In Outlook 2002, Tools → E-mail Accounts → View or change existing e-mail accounts → Next. Select an account and use Change → More Settings → Advanced → Leave a copy of messages on the server. You can also automatically delete them from the server after a set period or when you delete them from your Deleted Items folder.

In Outlook 2000, Tools → Accounts. Select an account and use Properties → Advanced → Leave a copy of messages on server. You can also automatically delete them from the server after a set period or when you delete them from your Deleted Items folder.

NOTE

This feature is often used by people who check their mail from different computers. Set up one computer to not leave a copy of messages on the server. Set up the other computers to leave a copy of messages on the server. The one computer that does not leave a copy will eventually end up with a copy of all messages received (including those you receive on other computers). There are also other, more elegant ways of checking an account from multiple computers. Check out *Outlook 2000 in a Nutshell*, by Tom Syroid and Bo Leuf (O'Reilly) for details on other methods.

Control when different accounts check for messages using Send/Receive groups?

This feature is available only in Outlook 2002. A Send/Receive group is a collection of email accounts that you can configure send and receive settings for as a group. For example, you could put some accounts into a group that automatically checks for new messages every five minutes and put the rest of your accounts into a group that checks for messages only when you tell it to. By default, a group named All Accounts is configured that contains all email accounts. Use Tools → Options → Mail Setup → Send/Receive (or Ctrl-Alt-S) to open the Send/Receive Groups dialog (Figure 3-1).

Click New to create a new group and choose which accounts should be in the group. Click Edit to modify settings for an existing group. Select a group and use the

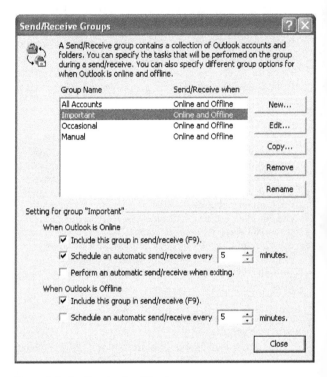

Figure 3-1. Configuring Send/Receive groups

settings at the bottom of the dialog to control whether the group is included when you click the Send/Receive button in Outlook (or use Tools → Send/Receive → Send and Receive All). You can also set up the group to automatically check mail every so many minutes and perform a Send/Receive when exiting. When you set up a bunch of custom groups, make sure you disable the settings for the All Accounts group.

Once you configure Send/Receive groups, any scheduled settings start working immediately. Commands are also added to the Tools → Send/Receive submenu for performing a manual send/receive on any group.

Have Outlook automatically check for messages at certain intervals?

In Outlook 2002, Tools → Options → Mail Setup → Send/Receive. Select the send/receive group (use All Accounts if you haven't set up custom groups), enable the "Schedule an automatic send/receive every" option, and set the time in minutes.

In Outlook 2000, Tools → Options → Mail Delivery → Check for new messages every.

Have Outlook warn me before it switches to a different dial-up connection?

In Outlook 2002, Tools → Options → Mail Setup → "Warn before switching an existing dial-up connection." You can also have Outlook always use an existing dial-up connection instead of switching.

In Outlook 2000, Tools → Options → Mail Delivery → "Warn before switching dial-up connection."

Have Outlook automatically hang up after checking for messages?

In Outlook 2002, Tools → Options → Mail Setup → "Hang up when finished with a manual Send/Receive."

In Outlook 2000, Tools → Options → Mail Delivery → "Hang up when finished sending, receiving, or updating."

Perform a Send/Receive to check all accounts for new messages and send all outgoing messages?

Tools → Send/Receive → Send and Receive All or press F9.

Click the Send/Receive button on the Standard toolbar when viewing an email folder.

Send outgoing messages without checking for new incoming messages?

Tools → Send/Receive → Send All.

Check for new messages only on a particular account?

Tools → Send/Receive. Click the account name.

Have Outlook display a notification message when new messages arrive?

Tools → Options → Preferences → E-mail Options → Display a notification when new mail arrives.

Have Outlook play a sound, change the mouse cursor, or show an envelope in the system tray when new messages arrive?

Tools → Options → Preferences → E-mail Options → Advanced E-Mail Options. Use the options in the "When new items arrive" section. Note that the "Show an envelope icon in the system tray" option is available only in Outlook 2002.

02+ *Manage an IMAP or web-based account?*

Since IMAP and web-based accounts use server-based storage, they are handled a little differently than POP3 accounts. While POP3 accounts deliver messages to the inbox in your Personal Folders, each IMAP and web-based account appears as a separate root folder equal to your Personal Folders (Figure 3-2). Each account has its own Inbox, Sent Items, and Deleted Items folder, along with other folders you create on the server.

For the most part, Outlook tries to make the functions in IMAP and web-based folders work the same as the mail folders in your Personal Folders. However, there are some quirks:

- You can download just the headers of messages without the message bodies. This lets you scan through messages and mark for download only the messages you actually want to read, saving time and bandwidth. Use the Tools → Send/Receive → Work with Headers submenu to find commands for using headers.

- You can work in the folders without connecting to the mail server, but you won't see new messages. To connect, use the File → Connect to command.

- For IMAP accounts, you can subscribe to particular folders. By default, only those folders you subscribe

---

Figure 3-2. IMAP and web-based accounts have their own sets of folders

to are shown in the Outlook view. The most common use for this feature is setting up an IMAP account as a public receptacle that contains many folders of information. To set this up, select the Inbox for the IMAP account and use Tools → IMAP Folders. Click Query to see the folders, or enter a part of a folder name and click Query to see a subset of folders.

NOTE

Outlook 2000 does not support web-based accounts. It does support IMAP accounts, but it does this so poorly that most people won't even use the feature. You can find out more about Outlook 2000's IMAP support from *Outlook 2000 in a Nutshell*, by Tom Syroid and Bo Leuf (O'Reilly). My advice, though, is to upgrade to Outlook 2002 or use other software if you need IMAP support.

Creating and Using Messages

Create a new message?

From any email folder, click the New Mail Message button on the Standard toolbar, press Ctrl-N, or select Actions → New Mail Message.

From any folder in Outlook, use File → New → Mail Message.

TIP

Copy any text or item to the Windows clipboard. Switch to Outlook and press Ctrl-V or use Edit → Paste. A new message window appears with the copied material in the message body.

Address a message to someone?

In an open message window (Figure 3-3), click the To button to open the address book and choose names. You can also start typing a name that you know is in your address book in any address field. Outlook 2002 will try to complete the name for you (or show you a list of possibilities if it can't decide which to use). Outlook 2000 works differently: when you leave the address field (by tabbing or clicking somewhere else), Outlook 2000 tries to figure out the name for you based on entries in the address book. If it finds a match (e.g., you typed "John" and there is only one John in the address book), it fills it in. If there are multiple matches, it places a red underline beneath the name. Right-click the name to see the alternate choices. A third method for addressing a message is just to type a full email address into the field. You can put multiple names or addresses (separated by semicolons or commas) into any address field.

Use the Cc and Bcc fields for a message?

The Cc field is used for sending a copy of a message to someone. The difference between the Cc and To fields is subjective. Cc is usually reserved for someone who needs

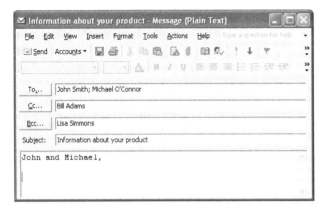

Figure 3-3. Addressing a new email message

a copy of the message but isn't the primary recipient who needs to act on the message.

The Bcc field is for blind copies. Other recipients of the message will not see the addresses you put into this field. Use it for sending copies of messages to people you don't want the primary recipients of the message to know about or have the addresses for.

Specify whether commas can be used to separate the addresses in a message?

   Tools → Options → Preferences → E-Mail Options → Advanced E-Mail Options → Allow comma as address separator.

Turn off automatic name checking?

   Tools → Options → Preferences → E-Mail Options → Advanced E-Mail Options → Automatic name checking.

Turn off automatic name completion?

   Tools → Options → Preferences → E-Mail Options → Advanced E-Mail Options → Suggest names while completing the To, Cc, and Bcc fields.

Create a new message by choosing a contact first?

From any contact folder (or an open contact), select the contacts (or group of contacts) and use Actions → New Message to Contact. You can also right-click a contact and choose New Message to Contact, or drag a contact to any email folder.

Create a message using another Outlook item?

Drag the item to any email folder, such as the inbox or outbox (e.g., drag a note to the Inbox). The exact effect depends on the type of item dragged. For most items, the subject is used as the subject of the email, and any text in the object is included in the body of the message.

Save a draft copy of a message?

A draft is automatically saved in the Drafts folder when a message is left open for a set amount of time (three minutes by default). You can also save a message by clicking the Save button (or using File → Save) on any open message window.

Change how often unfinished messages are saved?

Tools → Options → E-Mail Options → Advanced E-Mail Options → AutoSave unsent every *xx* minutes.

Change the folder to which unfinished messages are saved?

Tools → Options → E-Mail Options → Advanced E-Mail Options → Save unsent items in.

Change the priority of a new message?

In an open message window, click the Importance:High or Importance:Low buttons on the Standard toolbar (represented as an exclamation point and a down arrow, respectively). Selecting neither of these designates the message as Normal. The importance of an item is displayed next to an item in the inbox of the recipient.

In an open message window, click the Options button on the Standard toolbar and use the Importance drop-down list.

Change the default priority of all new messages?
> Tools → Options → E-Mail Options → Advanced E-Mail Options → Set importance.

Mark a sensitive message as private, personal, or confidential?
> In an open message window, click the Options button on the Standard toolbar and use the Sensitivity drop-down list.

Change the default sensitivity of all new messages?
> Tools → Options → E-Mail Options → Advanced E-Mail Options → Set sensitivity.

Have a message expire after a certain date?
> In an open message window, click the Options button on the Standard toolbar and use the "Expires after" option. An expired message is marked as expired at that time. When AutoArchive runs (see Part II for more), you have the option of automatically deleting expired items. A note at the top of the message lets the recipient know it's expired (if the recipient is using Outlook), and the message is also "struck through" in the Display pane.

Keep a message in my Outbox until a certain date?

 In an open message window, click the Options button on the Standard toolbar and use the "Do not deliver before" option.

Change whether copies of sent messages are saved in the Sent Items folder?
> Tools → Options → E-Mail Options → Save copies of messages in Sent Items folder.

Send a message I have sent before?
> Select the Sent Items folder and open the message you want to resend. Use Actions → Resend to send the message again (this is Outlook 2002 only). Use Actions → Resend This Message to edit the message before resending.

Recall a message I have already sent?

To use this feature, you must be using an Exchange server. Select the Sent Items folder and open the message you want to recall. Use Actions → Recall This Message. You are given the option to recall the message (which deletes it from the recipient's Inbox) or recall and replace the message with a new one.

Open a message?

Double-click the message.

Select the message (or messages) and use File → Open → Selected Items or press Ctrl-O.

Right-click the message and choose Open.

Read messages using the Preview pane?

View → Preview Pane or click the Preview Pane button on the Advanced toolbar. This pane appears under the view of messages and shows select headers and the body of the message.

View or hide the headers for messages in the Preview pane?

Double-click the blank area at the top of the Preview pane to show or hide common headers.

Change whether Outlook marks messages as read when viewing them in the preview pane?

Tools → Options → Other → Preview Pane → Mark messages as read in preview window. Set the number of seconds you must view a message in the preview pane before it is marked as read.

Have Outlook mark a message as read when I select another message?

Tools → Options → Other → Preview Pane → Mark item as read when selection changes.

Use just the spacebar to read all my messages with the Preview pane?

Tools → Options → Other → Preview Pane → Single key reading using space bar. When enabled, you can press the spacebar to scroll through a message in the Preview pane. When you get to the end of the message, pressing the spacebar moves to the next message.

Delete a message?
Select one or more messages. Choose Edit → Delete, press Ctrl-D, or press the Delete key.

Right-click any message or selected group of messages and choose Delete.

Drag a message or selected group of messages to the Deleted Items folder.

TIP

Hold the Shift key while deleting a message using any of the deletion methods (except Ctrl-D) to delete the message permanently instead of moving it to the Deleted Items folder.

Print a message?
Select a message or a group of messages. Choose File → Print, press Ctrl-P, press the Print button on the Standard toolbar, or right-click the task and choose Print.

Print messages automatically when they arrive?
Create a rule (see "Using Rules" later in this part).

Mark a message as read or unread?
Select the message (or messages) and use Edit → Mark as Read or Edit → Mark as Unread. Read messages have an open envelope icon. Unread messages have a closed envelope icon and are in bold text.

Reply to a message?
Select the message (or open a message window) and use Actions → Reply or click the Reply button on the Standard toolbar. Replying to a message automatically addresses the message to the person listed in the From header. By default, the contents of the original message are included in the body of the reply message.

To send a reply to all recipients listed in the From, To, and Cc fields (except for you, of course), use the Reply to All command.

Save the reply to a message in the folder with the original message instead of in the Sent Items folder?

By default, when you reply to a message, the reply is saved in the Sent Items folder, just like any other message you send. Instead, you can save the replies in the same folder as the message to which you are replying. The catch is that this works only when the original message is in a folder other than the Inbox. Use Tools → Options → E-Mail Options → Advanced E-Mail Options → In folders other than the Inbox, save replies with original message.

Forward a copy of a message to someone else?

Select the message (or open a message window) and use Actions → Forward or click the Forward button on the Standard toolbar.

Save a copy of forwarded messages in the Sent Items folder?

Tools → Options → E-Mail Options → Advanced E-Mail Options → Save forwarded messages. By default, forwarded messages are not saved (since you already have the original).

Control how Outlook handles the original message text when replying or forwarding?

Tools → Options → Preferences → E-mail Options. Set actions in the "When replying to a message" and "When forwarding a message" drop-down lists. If you select the "Prefix each line of the original message" option from either of these lists, you can control the prefix character (">" by default) using the "Prefix each line with" box.

Have Outlook mark my comments in a reply or forwarded message?

Tools → Options → Preferences → E-mail Options → Mark my comments with. After enabling the option,

---

change the text for marking comments using the box to the right of the option.

Use Microsoft Word as the editor for a new message, regardless of my default editor?
From any email folder, Actions → New Message Using → Microsoft Word (Plain Text).

Use Microsoft Word as the default editor for all new messages?
Tools → Options → Mail Format → Use Microsoft Word to edit e-mail messages.

NOTE

The advantage of using Word as an editor is that you get all its features—spellchecking, AutoText, enhanced formatting, and so on. The disadvantage is that it is a little cumbersome for sending quick messages. It also consumes more system resources to have two big programs running (Outlook and Word), though this is less of a problem in Outlook 2002 than in Outlook 2000.

Use Microsoft Word as the default viewer for all RTF messages?
Tools → Options → Mail Format → Use Microsoft Word to read Rich Text e-mail messages.

Specify the default message format for all new messages?
Tools → Options → Mail Format → Compose in this message format.

Create a single message using a specific format no matter what the default settings?
From any email folder, use one of the options on the Actions → New Mail Message Using submenu.

Specify the default format of all messages sent to a particular contact?
In Outlook 2002, open the contact, double-click the address in the E-mail address field, and choose a format using the Internet format field.

In Outlook 2000, open the contact and use the "Send using plain text" option under the E-mail address field. This is all the control you have in Outlook 2000.

02+ *Force Outlook to send RTF-formatted messages as RTF for all messages?*

By default, Outlook converts RTF-formatted messages to HTML format when it sends them. Change this using Tools → Options → Mail Format → Internet Format → Outlook Rich Text options.

Configure the fastest, simplest, most accepted format for sending messages?

There are so many formatting options—use Word as the editor, use plain text, use RTF, use HTML, set up different defaults for individual contacts—it's dizzying. Here's what I do:

- Set Outlook to use plain text by default (Tools → Options → Mail Format → Compose in this message format → Plain Text).
- Use the Outlook editor instead of Word (Tools → Options → Mail Format; clear all the Word options).

Don't bother setting defaults for individual contacts. It's confusing.

Plain text messages are fast, easy, and every email software out there can read them. They may not be sexy, but who cares? If you want to use a different format occasionally, use the Actions → New Mail Message Using menu to override the defaults for a single message.

By the way, when you reply to a message using a particular format (say, HTML), Outlook formats the reply using that format and ignores your default settings. Change the format of a reply by choosing another option from the Format menu of the reply window.

Change the character width at which Outlook wraps plain text messages?

Tools → Options → Mail Format → Internet Format → Automatically wrap text at.

Ask recipients of a particular message to return read or delivery receipts?

In the message window, click the Options button on the Standard toolbar and select the "Request a delivery receipt for this message" or "Request a read receipt for this message" option—or both. Recipients are prompted with a pop-up window asking them to return a receipt. They usually have the option of honoring the receipt or not.

Ask recipients of all messages to return read or delivery receipts?

Tools → Options → E-Mail Options → Tracking Options. Select the "Read receipt" and "Delivery receipt" options.

WARNING

The fact is, requests for receipts are annoying because it's one more thing that gets in your way when reading your mail. Some people even find them insulting. My advice is don't enable receipts for all messages unless you are required to for some reason.

Have Outlook automatically return read and delivery receipts?

Tools → Options → E-Mail Options → Tracking Options → Always send a response. You can also have Outlook never send a response.

Have replies to a message sent to someone else?

When creating a new message, use Options → Have replies sent to.

Add voting buttons to a message?

When creating a new message, use Options → Use voting buttons. Use the drop-down list to select the buttons

---

that should appear. Buttons for the vote appear on the
message window. When the recipient clicks a button, a
message with the vote is returned to you. This requires
that both parties use Outlook.

Track the results of a vote?

Open the original message from the Sent Items folder.
Click the Tracking tab to see the votes. The Tracking tab
does not appear on messages in plain text format.
Instead, text that indicates the vote status appears on the
header. You can click the text to open an RTF-formatted
version of the message and see the Tracking tab.

Viewing Messages

Sort messages by their follow-up flags?

View → Current View → By Follow-up Flag or use the
Current View drop-down list on the Advanced toolbar.

Sort messages by their sender?

View → Current View → By Sender or use the Current
View drop-down list on the Advanced toolbar.

Sort messages by who they were sent to?

View → Current View → Sent To or use the Current View
drop-down list on the Advanced toolbar.

View messages by subject?

View → Current View → By Conversation Topic or use
the Current View drop-down list on the Advanced toolbar. This is an especially useful view for folders that contain messages from a mailing list or discussion group.

View only unread messages?

View → Current View → Unread Messages or use the
Current View drop-down list on the Advanced toolbar.

View only messages from the last seven days?

View → Current View → Last Seven Days or use the Current View drop-down list on the Advanced toolbar.

View messages on a timeline?

   View → Current View → Message Timeline or use the
   Current View drop-down list on the Advanced toolbar.

Show week numbers when viewing messages on a timeline?

   View → Current View → Customize Current View →
   Other Settings → Show week numbers. You can also
   right-click any blank space in the view and choose Other
   Settings → Show week numbers.

Change the width of labels on messages in timeline view?

   View → Current View → Customize Current View →
   Other Settings → Maximum label width. You can also
   right-click any blank space in the view and choose Other
   Settings → Maximum label width.

*View a three-line AutoPreview of messages in the Display
pane?*

   View → AutoPreview (Figure 3-4).

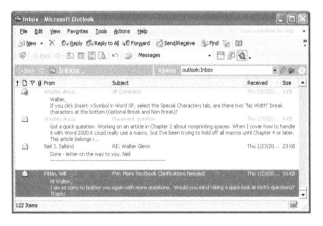

*Figure 3-4. AutoPreview shows the first three lines of a message in
the Display pane*

Change whether AutoPreview works on all messages or just unread messages?

View → Current View → Customize Current View → Other Settings. Choose the "Preview all items" or "Preview unread items" options. Choosing No AutoPreview is the same as turning it off using View → AutoPreview.

Change the subject of a message I've received?

Open the message and edit the subject field, even though it looks like it can't be edited. This can be a handy way of keeping messages on the same subject together, even when the sender uses a different subject.

Allow editing of message fields directly in a table view?

View → Current View → Customize Current View → Other Settings → Allow in-cell editing. You can also right-click any blank space in the view and choose Other Settings → Allow in-cell editing. You can't change fields you couldn't change already by opening the window, but this feature works well in combination with the previous task for quickly renaming subjects.

Attaching Items to Messages

Attach a file to a message?

In a new message window, use Insert → File or click the Insert File button on the Standard toolbar. Browse for the file to attach. You can select several files to attach at once.

You can also drag files from Windows straight onto an open message window to attach them.

Use an attachment from a message I've received?

Messages with attachments have a paperclip icon in the
Display pane. Open a message, and the attachments are
displayed along with the headers. Double-click the
attachment to open it or right-click it for other options
(Print, Save As, etc.).

Insert an Outlook item into the body of a message?

In a new message window, use Insert → Item.

Insert a picture into the body of a message?

Create a new HTML format message. In the open message window, use Insert → Picture.

Include a URL in the body of a message?

Type the URL. Outlook automatically formats it as a
hyperlink.

Insert a web page as the body of a message?

Open the page in your web browser. Select the entire
page (most browsers have a Select All command on the
Edit menu). Paste the page into your message body.

If you're using Microsoft Internet Explorer, open the
page and use File → Send → Page by E-Mail.

Using Signatures and Stationery

Stationery is a template or form with which you can preformat messages that you might send more than once so that you don't have to retype information for each message.

Use stationery on a message?
> Actions → New Mail Message Using → More Stationery. Select a stationery from the dialog that opens and click OK. Recently used stationery appears directly on the Actions → New Mail Message Using submenu.

WARNING

Stationery requires an HTML-formatted message. Aside from the other reasons not to use HTML messages (bigger messages, etc.), people who have email software that doesn't display them (or is set not to) might have trouble seeing your message. Also, it's harder to read text against most stationery than against a plain white background anyway.

Specify the default stationery used for new messages?
> Tools → Options → Mail Format → Use this stationery by default. This option is unavailable unless you also select the HTML format as your default on this same dialog. Use the Stationery Picker button to browse the stationery before choosing it.

Create a message without stationery when a default stationery is enabled?
> From any mail folder, Actions → New Mail Message Using. Choose Plain Text, Rich Text, or HTML (No Stationery).

Create stationery?
> Tools → Options → Mail Format → Stationery Picker → New.

Edit an existing stationery?

Tools → Options → Mail Format → Stationery Picker. Select a stationery and click Edit.

Delete a stationery?

Tools → Options → Mail Format → Stationery Picker. Select a stationery and click Remove.

Create a signature for email messages?

Tools → Options → Mail Format → Signatures → New. A wizard walks you through creating the signature. You can type it yourself from scratch, use an existing signature as a template, or use a text file as a template.

Insert a signature in an email message?

Start a new message. In the message window, use the Insert → Signature submenu.

NOTE

If you are using Microsoft Word as your email editor, signatures are more complicated. In a new message window, click the down arrow next to the Options button on the Standard toolbar (the one at the bottom with the Send button on it). Choose E-Mail signature. Select a signature, copy it, and paste it into the message body. You also have the option of setting up AutoText signatures in Microsoft Word, which is easier if you plan to use Word regularly as an editor.

Specify the default signature used for all email messages?

Tools → Options → Mail Format.

In Outlook 2002, you can choose one default signature for new messages and one for replies and forwards.

In Outlook 2000, you can set a default for all messages and then elect not to include it on replies and forwards.

Change an existing signature?

Tools → Options → Mail Format → Signatures. Select the signature and click Edit.

Delete a signature?
> Tools → Options → Mail Format → Signatures. Select the signature and click Remove.

Include a vCard with my signature?
> Tools → Options → Mail Format → Signatures. Create a new email signature or edit an existing one. On the Edit Signature dialog, use the vCard options section to pick an existing vCard or create a new one from a contact. (See Part V for more on vCards.)

Managing Messages

Create a new mail folder?
> File → New → Folder. Enter a folder name, select Mail and Post Items for its contents, choose where to place the folder, and click OK.

Move messages to a different folder?
> Drag the messages to the new folder using the Folder List or the Outlook Bar.
>
> Select the messages and use Edit → Move to Folder or press Ctrl-Shift-V.
>
> Right-click the message and choose Move to Folder.

Assign a category to a message?
> Select the message and choose Edit → Categories. You can also right-click a message and choose Categories.
>
> For a new message you're creating, click the Options button on the Standard toolbar and then click Categories.

Assign a contact to a message?
> Right-click the message and choose Options. Use the Contacts button.
>
> For a new message you're creating, click the Options button on the Standard toolbar and then click Contacts.

Flag a message for follow up?

Select the message and use Actions → Follow Up or press Ctrl-Shift-G.

Right-click the message and choose Follow Up.

Add a reminder to a flagged message?

Flag a message for follow up and set a due date. The reminder pops up at the due date.

For a message that's already flagged, select it and press Ctrl-Shift-G to open the Flag for Follow up window. You can also open the message and click the Follow Up button on the Standard toolbar.

Set a priority for a message I've received?

Open the message and use View → Options → Importance.

Right-click the message and use Options → Importance.

View all Internet headers for a message?

Open the message and use View → Options → Internet Headers. (See Part IX for explanations of Internet headers.)

Right-click the message, use Options → Internet Headers.

Find all messages related to a selected message?

Open the message and use Actions → Find All → Related Messages. This searches all Personal Folders for messages with similar subjects.

Right-click the message and use Find All → Related Messages.

Find all messages from the same sender as a selected message?

Open the message and use Actions → Find All → Messages from Sender. This searches for all Personal Folders messages from the same sender.

Right-click the message and use Find All → Messages from Sender.

Using Rules

Rules (like filters) let Outlook automatically process messages as they come into your Inbox (or when they go to your Outbox) and do things with those messages—lots of things. Though there are many options, there are four sets of questions you should ask with regards to any rule:

- Should the rule apply to incoming or outgoing messages?

- What conditions make the rule applicable? Messages from a certain person? With certain words in the subject? That come through a certain account? There are many choices. You can even apply multiple conditions.

- What should Outlook do with messages that meet the conditions? Move them to a folder? Assign them a category? Delete them? Mark them as Important? Again, there are many options, and you can assign multiple actions.

- Are there exceptions? Don't apply the rule if the message is marked important? If it comes from a specific person?

This section only provides pointers for where to go to perform actions. Rules systems can become so complicated that I just can't fully cover them in a book like this. For more details and some good advice, check out Tom Syroid's *Outlook 2000 in a Nutshell* (O'Reilly).

Create a new rule from scratch?
    Tools → Rules Wizard → New → Start from a blank rule.

Create a new rule based on a template?
    Tools → Rules Wizard → New → Start creating a rule from a template.

Create a rule based on a message?
    Right-click the message and choose New Rule.

Turn a rule on or off?
    Tools → Rules Wizard. Click the checkbox next to a rule in the list. When a rule is turned on, it runs automatically.

Change a rule?

Tools → Rules Wizard. Select a rule and click Modify.

Change the order in which rules are applied?

Tools → Rules Wizard. Select a rule and click Move Up or Move Down. The order in which rules are applied is extremely important.

Copy a rule?

Tools → Rules Wizard. Select a rule and click Copy. Use this if an existing rule almost meets your needs and needs only a couple of tweaks.

Delete a rule?

Tools → Rules Wizard. Select a rule and click Delete.

Import or export rules?

Tools → Rules Wizard → Options. Use the import and export options to back up rules, restore rules from a backup, or move them to another computer. Rules are saved as *.rwz* files.

Run rules manually (and even on a different folder than the Inbox)?

Tools → Rules Wizard → Run Now. Select the rules to run and click Run Now. You can also specify the folder in which the rules will be applied. The default is the folder that was selected when you started the Rules Wizard.

Taming Junk Email

Outlook includes a rudimentary Junk E-Mail feature. Basically, it keeps a list of addresses (it starts with some and you add others) and looks for certain word patterns. If it detects a junk email (these unsolicited and unwanted messages are frequently called "spam"), Outlook moves the items to a special folder or deletes them (your option). While this feature may work well for some people, there are better options available. Check out *http://www.cloudmark.com* for one of the best and easiest options (and it's free).

Automatically color junk messages?

Tools → Organize. In the Organize pane that opens above the Display pane, click Junk E-Mail. For some reason, Outlook has separate options for junk messages and adult content. Select the Color option in the first drop-down list for each item, select the color, and click the appropriate Turn on button.

Automatically move junk messages?

Tools → Organize → Junk E-Mail. Select the Move option in the first drop-down list for each item, select the folder (the new Junk E-Mail folder created by default should be just fine), and click the appropriate Turn on button.

NOTE

Both the automatic-coloring and automatic-moving features turn on rules that you can view using Tools → Rules Wizard.

Change the folder junk email is sent to?

Tools → Organize → Junk E-Mail. Click the second drop-down list for each item (junk and adult content) and choose Deleted Items (to simply delete them) or Other Folder.

View the junk senders list?

Tools → Organize → Junk E-Mail. At the bottom of the Organize pane, click the "Click here" link. Click Edit Junk Senders or Edit Adult Content Senders.

Download updates for the junk senders list?

Tools → Organize → Junk E-Mail. At the bottom of the Organize pane, click the "Click here" link. Click Outlook Web Site.

Add a sender to the junk senders list?

Select the message from the sender and use Actions → Junk E-Mail. You can add the sender to either the junk senders or adult content senders list.

TIP

One simple way of reducing the amount of junk email you get is to create a rule that moves all incoming messages to a different folder unless they have your name or address in the To or Cc line. Spammers often send messages to a list, meaning that your address won't actually appear. Create a rule that moves all messages coming in through your account to a folder (name it "suspect" or something similar). Add two exceptions to the rule: "except where my name is in the To box" and "except where my name is in the Cc box." You'll need to create a rule for each account you have.

Edit the exceptions list for junk senders?

Tools → Rules Wizard. Select the Exception list rule and click the Exception List link in the Rule description box. Use the dialog that opens to add or remove senders to the exception list. Use this list if you find senders that are being tagged as junk senders but shouldn't be.

PART IV

Calendar Tasks

This part covers using Outlook's Calendar to keep track of your time—and other people's time if you need to. Tasks are divided into the following three categories:

- Creating and managing calendar items
- Planning meetings and using group views
- Changing calendar views

Within these categories, tasks are presented as answers to "How do I..." questions (e.g., "How do I save a personal calendar as a web page?"), followed by concise instructions for completing the task.

Creating and Managing Calendar Items

Create an appointment?

Switch to a calendar folder and click the New Appointment button on the Standard toolbar, or choose File → New → Appointment.

Double-click any blank area in the Display pane of a task folder. If you do this, the window defaults to creating an event. Disable the "All day event" option to turn it into an appointment.

You can also right-click the blank area and choose New Appointment.

Create a multi-day appointment?

Create an appointment that occurs at the same time over consecutive days by first creating an appointment. In the appointment window (Figure 4-1), set the start and end times and the start and end dates.

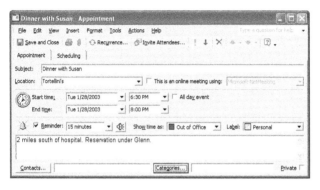

Figure 4-1. Creating a new appointment or event

Create an all-day (or multi-day) event?

Create an appointment using any of the methods already described. In the appointment window, select the "All day event" option. For a multi-day event (such as a vacation), just set the end time to the last day of the event.

NOTE

As you've probably noticed, the same form is used for the major calendar items: appointments and events. The difference is in the start and end times and whether the "All day event" option is set. You can convert one type of item to another by opening it and changing these settings.

Open a calendar item?

Double-click the item.

Select the item. Use File → Open → Selected Items, press Enter, or press Ctrl-O.

Right-click the item and choose Open.

Delete a calendar item?

Select one or more items. Choose Edit → Delete, press Ctrl-D, or press the Delete key.

Right-click any item or selected group of items and choose Delete.

Drag an item or selected group of items to the Deleted Items folder.

NOTE

Hold the Shift key while deleting a calendar item using any of the deletion methods (except Ctrl-D) to delete the item permanently instead of moving it to the Deleted Items folder.

Make a calendar item a recurring option?

In any open calendar item window, click the Recurrence button on the Standard toolbar to open the Appointment Recurrence dialog (Figure 4-2). Set a start and end time (or a duration). Choose whether the appointment should appear Daily, Weekly, Monthly, or Yearly, and then set the recurrence schedule (for example, Weekly every Tuesday). Set a range of recurrence to determine how far into the future recurrences should be created. Once you click OK, an appointment is created on each date of the recurrence in your calendar.

Create a new recurring item from any calendar view?

Right-click a day or time (depending on your current view) in the Display pane and choose New Recurring Appointment (or Event or Meeting). This creates a new calendar item and automatically opens the Appointment Recurrence dialog with the proper day or time already set.

Delete a specific instance of a recurring item?

Use any normal method for deleting the item (right-click and choose Delete, drag it to Deleted Items, etc.). Outlook opens a dialog asking whether to delete just that instance or the entire series.

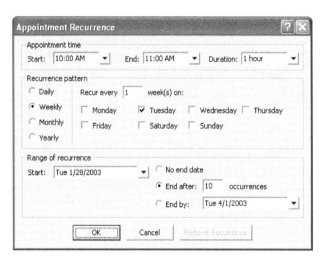

Figure 4-2. Creating a recurring appointment

Delete a whole series of recurring items?

Use any normal method for deleting the item, and Outlook opens a dialog asking whether to delete just that instance or the entire series.

You can also open an instance of the item, click Recurrence, and then click Remove Recurrence on the Appointment Recurrence dialog (Figure 4-2). This method saves the earliest instance of the item but removes all others.

Mark a calendar item as private?

Open any calendar item and select Private. This is useful for hiding items in shared folders.

Add holidays to my Calendar?

Tools → Options → Calendar Options → Add Holidays.

Manage holiday lists and find updated lists?

Outlook imports holidays from a text file named *outlook.txt* (in Outlook 2000) or *outlook.hol* (in Outlook 2002). These are in the *Program Files\ Microsoft Office\Office10\1033* folder (Office instead of Office10 for Outlook 2000). You can modify this text file to create custom holidays. Outlook 2000 users may notice that their holidays expire at the end of 2002. You can download an updated list from *http://www.officeupdate.com*.

Set a reminder?

In an open calendar item window, select the Reminder option. By default, a reminder window will pop up 15 minutes before the start time of the appointment. Change this time using the drop-down list to the right of the Reminder option. You can also type a time directly into the box.

Change whether a reminder is automatically set for all new calendar events?

Tools → Options → Preferences → Default reminder. Use the drop-down list to the right of the option to specify the default lead time.

Change (or turn off) the reminder sounds for a particular calendar item?

Open the calendar item and click the Sound button to the right of the Reminder option. Choose whether to play a sound or browse for a new *.wav* file to play. This setting affects only the open calendar item.

> *Change (or turn off) the reminder sounds for all reminders in Outlook?*
>
> Tools → Options → Other → Advanced Options → Reminder Options → Play Reminder sound. Turn the option on or off, or Browse for a different *.wav* file to play. This setting affects reminders for all items in Outlook—not just calendar items. Reminders still open; you are just changing the sound.

Save an appointment in iCalendar or vCalendar format?

In an open appointment window, choose File → Save As. Select iCalendar Format (*.ics*) or vCalendar Format (*.vcs*). Both of these formats are intended to make it easy to exchange calendar information between different types of software. Unfortunately, they are not very well-supported.

Save a personal calendar as a web page?

Select the calendar view you want to save and click File → Save as Web Page. Set details such as start and end date, whether appointments should be listed, a page title, and a location to save the files (a default location is specified, but you must add a filename to the end of it). Click Save. If the "Open saved web page in browser" option is selected, you'll see the page immediately.

Planning Meetings and Using Group Views

A meeting is an appointment to which you invite other people; it can happen in person or it can happen online using Microsoft NetMeeting. If invitees accept the invitation, it becomes an appointment in their calendars. Every meeting has an organizer (the person who plans it), attendees (the people invited), and, optionally, some scheduled resources (e.g., a room or a projector). When you organize a meeting, invitations go out via email and you receive responses in your Inbox.

Group schedules are new to Outlook 2002 and provide an easy way to view calendar information for more than one person at a time. In fact, you can set up multiple group schedules at once for different groups or departments.

Both scheduling meetings and creating group schedules happen only if you can access scheduling information from another person's computer (called free/busy information). If you're on a company network, this may already be set up for you. Otherwise, you'll need to either set it up on your network or use a service like the Microsoft Office Internet Free/Busy service (free for users of Outlook 2002). Outlook 2002 actually prompts you to sign up the first time you view a meeting schedule if you don't have another service configured.

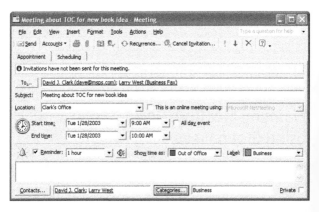

Figure 4-3. Sending a simple meeting request

Schedule a quick meeting?
　　From any calendar folder, Actions → New Meeting Request. From any folder, you can use File → New →

Meeting Request. This opens a new Meeting dialog (Figure 4-3). Click the To button on the Meeting dialog box to choose who to invite. The To dialog lets you specify whether each invitee is required to attend or just requested. Click Send to add the appointment to your calendar and send the invitations out via email. This quick method does not require you to have access to other users' free/busy information, but it can also take a lot of back and forth emails before a time is agreed upon by all.

Use a distribution list to schedule a meeting?

 If you often schedule meetings with the same people, set up a distribution list with those people as members. (See Part V for more about distribution lists.) Then, just send the meeting request to the distribution list. If you want to send requests to only part of the distribution list, switch over to the Scheduling tab and click the small plus sign to the left of the distribution list. After confirming, Outlook expands the list to display all the listed members instead of just the list name. Remove the members you don't want to invite.

Use a meeting request I have received?

Open the meeting request like any other email. Click Accept, Decline, or Tentative.

Outlook 2002 adds an additional option: Propose New Meeting Time. When proposing a new time, you can even use the free/busy information of the other attendees to help you plan the new time.

Track responses to meetings I have requested?

Open the appointment for the meeting and switch to the Tracking tab. This tab lists each invitee, whether they are required or requested at the meeting, and any responses you have received from them.

Invite other people to a meeting I've already scheduled?
    Open the appointment for the meeting and switch to the Scheduling tab. Click Invite Others to generate new email invitations.

Update a meeting request?
    If you need to change the meeting time, location, or other details, do so by opening and editing your appointment for the meeting. On the Standard toolbar of the meeting window, click Send Update to send updated details to all attendees via email.

Cancel a meeting?
    Open the appointment for a meeting and choose Actions → Cancel Meeting. All attendees are notified via email.

Schedule resources for a meeting?
    This feature works only if you are connected to a Microsoft Exchange Server organization, which may be the case if you are on a company network. A resource is something like a room, a projector, or even an instructor. Resources (which are set up on an Exchange Server, remember) are available through the Address Book and are set up just like any other invitee. When you click the To button to decide who to invite, find the resource and invite it by selecting it and clicking Resources (Figure 4-4).

Set up a resource so it can be scheduled for meetings?
    Tools → Options → Calendar Options → Resource Scheduling. Note that this function first requires that your organization use Exchange Server and second, that you are set up as a resource administrator (which requires the actions of a network administrator).

Schedule an online meeting?
    Schedule a meeting using any of the normal methods. In the meeting window, select "This is an online meeting using." From the drop-down list, choose the software for hosting the meeting. Microsoft NetMeeting is used by default.

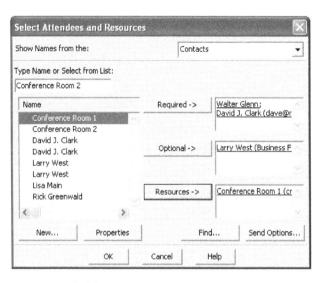

Figure 4-4. Scheduling a resource

Plan a meeting by first checking other people's schedules?

Schedule the meeting as already discussed. Once you have added the attendees, but before sending the message, switch to the Scheduling tab of the Meeting window (Figure 4-5). Outlook automatically searches the network for free/busy information on each attendee and displays it on the timeline. If a member cannot be found on the network, Outlook prompts you to sign up for the free Microsoft Office Internet Free/Busy service and offers to place a link in the meeting request so attendees can also sign up. Use the Add Others button to add people to the meeting. Use the Display pane to find free time for the meeting, or click AutoPick Next to jump to the next time when all attendees are free.

There is another way to plan a meeting. From any calendar window, use Actions → Plan a Meeting. This opens a

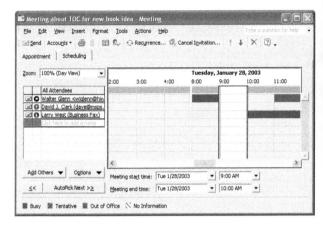

Figure 4-5. Planning a meeting

dialog that looks much like the scheduling tab of a meeting window. Configure it the same way and, when you're ready, click Make Meeting to send out the invitations.

Show pop-up calendar details when I'm scheduling a meeting?
Tools → Options → Calendar Options → Planner Options → Meeting Planner → Show popup calendar details.

Show calendar details in the grid when I am scheduling a meeting?
Tools → Options → Calendar Options → Planner Options → Meeting Planner → Show calendar details in the grid.

View counterproposals for a proposed meeting?
Open the meeting request, switch to the Scheduling tab, and look under Proposed Dates and Times. Pick a proposed time that works and click Send Update to update all the attendees with the new time.

Choose whether attendees can send counterproposals?
Tools → Options → Calendar Options → "Allow attendees to propose new times for meetings you organize."

Change the response given when I propose a new meeting time?
Tools → Options → Calendar Options → "Use this response when you propose new meeting times."

Create a group schedule?
From any calendar folder, use Actions → View Group Schedules → New. Type a name for the group and click OK. A window for the group schedule opens immediately.

NOTE

Group schedule windows look and act a lot like the Scheduling tab on a meeting window and the Plan Meeting dialog (see Figure 4-5). Add members in the same way. Pick members and click Make Meeting to schedule a meeting with those members. The advantage of using group schedules is that you can save multiple groups and view them whenever you want, without having to plan a meeting.

View a group schedule?
From any calendar folder, use Actions → View Group Schedules. Select a group and click open (or double-click the group).

Delete a group schedule?
From any calendar folder, use Actions → View Group Schedules. Select a group and click Delete.

Show pop-up calendar details when setting up a group schedule?
Tools → Options → Calendar Options → Planner Options → Group Schedule → Show popup calendar details.

Show calendar details in a grid when setting up a group schedule?

Tools → Options → Calendar Options → Planner Options → Group Schedule → Show calendar details in grid.

Send a meeting request from a group schedule?

From an open group schedule window, click Make Meeting and choose an option from the drop-down menu.

Customize a group schedule?

On any group schedule window, you can use the Options drop-down menu to show only working hours, show calendar details (actual appointments), and refresh the free/busy information for the members.

Publish a schedule?

If you are in an Exchange Server organization (used on company networks, mostly), your free/busy time is automatically made available to others. If not, you'll have to make that information available by publishing it to either the Microsoft Office Internet Free/Busy Service (available only for Outlook 2002) or to a specified Internet or intranet location. Free/busy information is published as a *.vbf* file that other Outlook users can access.

Configure this by using Tools → Options → Calendar Options → Free-Busy Options. You can specify the range of dates to publish, how often to update, and the location where the information should be published.

Change how free/busy information for a calendar item is shown to other people looking at your calendar?

Open the calendar item and use the "Show time as" drop-down list.

Changing Calendar Views

View a calendar folder using a day/week/month view?

With any calendar folder selected, use View → Current View → Day/Week/Month (or Day/Week/Month With AutoPreview). Once you're in a day/week/month view, use buttons on the Standard toolbar to switch between viewing a single day, a work week, a full week, or a month. Figure 4-6 shows a typical week view.

Figure 4-6. Viewing a week in Calendar

Use the Date Navigator?

In day, work week, and week views, a small calendar called the Date Navigator appears in the upper-right corner. Depending on how much room you give it (by dragging the vertical divider between it and the main view), you'll see one, two, or even more months. Figure 4-7 is a closer look at the Date Navigator. You can also drag the divider between the Date Navigator and TaskPad to increase or decrease the room given to either one.

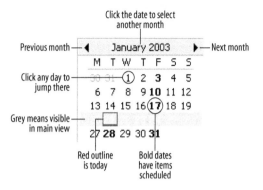

Figure 4-7. Deciphering the Date Navigator

View a different number of days than the default choices?

Drag to select any number of days on the Date Navigator. The main view changes to show these days. Selecting any number of days under six uses a work week–style view.

Change whether days with calendar items are bold in the Date Navigator?

View → Current View → Customize Current View → Other Settings → Bolded dates in Date Navigator represent days containing items. You can also get to the Other Settings dialog by right-clicking in the main view and choosing Other Settings.

Show week numbers in the Date Navigator?

Tools → Options → Calendar Options → Show week numbers in the Date Navigator. Numbers appear at the left edge.

Change the TaskPad view?

The TaskPad is a miniature representation of your task list, shown in most day/week/month views just under the Date Navigator. (See Figure 4-6.) By default, the Task-

---

Pad shows all tasks. Use options on the View → TaskPad View submenu to change the tasks displayed.

Change the alignment of tasks in the TaskPad?
Right-click the column header at the top of the TaskPad and select an option from the Alignment submenu.

Show the TaskPad and Date Navigator in Month view?
By default, these items are hidden in the Month view, but the vertical drag bar is hiding at the right edge of the view. Move your pointer just to the right of the vertical scrollbar until it turns into a drag icon, and then drag the bar to the left.

View an entire year?

For some reason, a year view is not built into Outlook 2000 or 2002. Go to View → Current View → Define Views. Click New. Name the new view "Year" (or whatever), select Day/Week/Month as the type of view, and click OK. Click Apply View. You should now be looking at your new Year view, which (at the moment) looks just like a day/week/month view. Size the Date Navigator so that it takes up the entire screen. That should give you one year of monthly calendars.

Go to a specific date?
Click the date in Date Navigator.

Use View → Go To → Go To Date. Type in the exact date.

Right-click in any view and choose Go to Date.

Add a color label to a calendar item?
Open the item and select an option from the Label drop-down list. Each color is associated with a particular subject (for example, light green is personal).

Right-click an item and choose an option from the Labels submenu.

Adding color to a recurring item adds color to every item in the series.

Edit the labels used with item colors?

Right-click an item and choose Labels → Edit Labels.

Have Outlook color calendar items automatically?

Right-click the calendar view and choose Automatic Formatting. Click Add. Type a name for the new rule and choose a label. Click Condition and use the dialog that opens to enter conditions (such as words found in the subject or attendees of the meeting). For example, you could have all meetings proposed by "John Smith" automatically color-coded as important.

Show time on calendar views as clocks?

From any day/week/month view, use View → Current View → Customize Current View → Other Settings. You can also right-click the view and choose Other Settings to get there faster. For the week and month views, enable the "Show time as clocks" options to have Outlook put small clocks next to the calendar items that display the correct time. Use the "Show end time" options to specify whether two clocks should be shown—one for the start time and one for the end time.

Change the default time scale for the day view?

View → Current View → Customize Current View → Other Settings → Time Scale.

Right-click the time scale (to the left of the main view) and choose one of the time options (60 minutes, 30 minutes, etc.) from the shortcut menu.

Change the time zone displayed in the day and work week views?

Tools → Options → Calendar Options → Time Zone. Enter an optional label for the time zone and choose the zone from the drop-down list. You can also right-click the vertical timeline at the left of the day and work week views and choose Change Time Zone to access the same dialog box.

Add an additional time zone to the day and work week views?
> Tools → Options → Calendar Options → Time Zone → Show an additional time zone.

Change the days in my work week?
> Tools → Options → Calendar Options. Select the days at the top of the dialog (Figure 4-8) that should be considered as part of the work week.

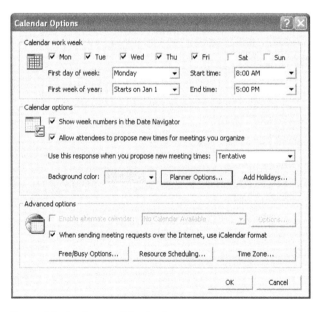

Figure 4-8. Configuring Calendar Options

Change the first day of the week?
> Tools → Options → Calendar Options → First day of week. This affects the day that appears first in week, work week, and month views.

Change the first week of the year?
> Tools → Options → Calendar Options → First week of year. This option affects only week numbering.

Change the start and end times of a work day?
> Tools → Options → Calendar Options → Start time and End time.

Set the background color for day and work week views?
> Tools → Options → Calendar Options → Background color.

Change whether weekend days are shown on a single column in month view?
> View → Current View → Customize Current View → Other Settings → Compress Weekend Days.
>
> Right-click the view, choose Other Settings → Compress Weekend Days.

View a list of active appointments?
> View → Current View → Active Appointments. You can also use the Current View drop-down menu on the Advanced toolbar to select this view and any of the following views.

View a list of events?
> View → Current View → Events.

View a list of annual events?
> View → Current View → Annual Events.

View a list of recurring appointments?
> View → Current View → Recurring Appointments.

View calendar items in the Preview pane?
> View → Preview Pane. Selected items are shown in the Preview pane but cannot be edited there.

PART V

Contacts Tasks

This section of the book covers using Outlook contacts for keeping track of the people in your life. Tasks are divided into the following four categories:

- Creating and editing contacts
- Using contacts
- Linking contacts with other items
- Changing contact views

Within these categories, tasks are presented as answers to "How do I..." questions (e.g., "How do I create a custom contact field?"), followed by concise instructions for completing the task.

Creating and Editing Contacts

Create a contact?

Switch to a contact folder and click the New Contact button on the Standard toolbar, choose File → New → Contact, or press Ctrl-N.

Double-click any blank area in the Display pane of a contact folder. You can also right-click the area and choose New Contact.

In some table views, a blank field labeled "Click here to add a new Contact" appears at the top of the list. Click it and start typing.

Create a new contact in the default Contacts folder without leaving the folder I'm in?

Select File → New → Contact—no matter what folder you're viewing. You can also click the down arrow next to the New button on the Standard toolbar.

Open an existing contact?

Double-click the contact.

Select the contact. Use File → Open → Selected Items, press the Enter key, or press Ctrl-O.

Right-click the contact and choose Open.

Delete a contact?

Select one or more contacts. Choose Edit → Delete, press Ctrl-D, or press the Delete key.

Right-click any contact or selected group of contacts and choose Delete.

Drag a contact or selected group of contacts to the Deleted Items folder.

TIP

Hold the Shift key while deleting a contact using any of these methods (except Ctrl-D) to delete the task permanently instead of moving it to the Deleted Items folder.

Print a contact?

Select a contact (or group of contacts). Choose File → Print, press Ctrl-P, press the Print button on the Standard toolbar, or right-click the contact and choose Print.

Configure the name of a person on the contact form?

In an open contact window (Figure 5-1), type the contact's name in the Full Name field. Outlook parses the name and tries to format it correctly (e.g., it turns "mike jones" into "Mike Jones"). Click the Full Name button to open a dialog where you can configure the name more precisely.

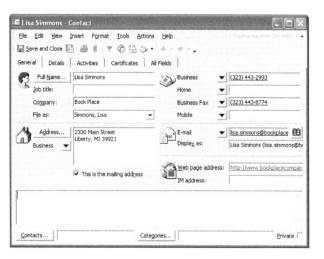

Figure 5-1. Creating a new contact

TIP

Outlook recognizes two names in the full name field if they are separated by "and" or "&". For example, you could enter "John & Debbie Smith". It will also recognize "The Smiths".

Change the order for how Outlook creates full names?

Tools → Options → Contact Options → Default "Full Name" Order.

Enter a phone number on a contact form?

As you enter the number into one of the phone fields, Outlook formats it for you. For example, 2565553425 would be converted to (256) 555-3425. For more control, press the Edit button (it looks like a pencil) that appears to the right of any phone field when you click to type in it.

Enter more phone numbers than the ones shown on the contact form?

Click the down arrow to the left of a phone field to choose from 19 different types of phone (and similarly formatted) fields. These settings are only for the current contact.

Enter more than one email address for a contact?

Click the down arrow to the left of the E-mail address field. You can enter three addresses per contact (labeled E-mail, E-Mail 2, and E-Mail 3).

NOTE

If one contact has multiple email addresses and you create a message to that contact, all addresses are included on the To line. You can delete the ones you don't want. If you create a message to multiple contacts, only the primary email address of each contact is used. For this reason, it might be better to create multiple contacts (such as "John at home" and "John at work") than to use multiple email addresses in a single contact.

Specify that Outlook send messages to a contact in plain text?

In Outlook 2000, open the contact and select the "Send using plain text" option under the E-mail address field.

In Outlook 2002, open the contact and double-click the email address in the E-mail field to open the E-mail Properties dialog. From the Internet format drop-down list, choose "Send plain text only." You can also specify that messages to the contact should be formatted using rich text format or that Outlook should decide which format to use.

Enter a contact's mailing address?

On the contact form, use the down arrow to the left of the Address box to choose Business, Home, or Other address—*then* enter the address into the field. Outlook tries to format the address for you. Click the Address button to control exactly how it is formatted.

Specify which address is the mailing address for a contact?

Choose the address using the down arrow to the left of the Address field and select the "This is the mailing address" option. Only one of these can be the mailing address at a time. The mailing address is used when creating letters to a contact or performing a mail merge.

Associate categories with a contact?

Select a contact and choose Edit → Categories.

Right-click a contact and choose Categories.

Open a contact and use the Categories button.

Associate other contacts with a contact?

In an open contact window, click Contacts to open a dialog for associating contacts.

Enter additional personal details for a contact?

In an open contact window, switch to the Details tab for fields like Department, Spouse's Name, Nickname, and more.

Store and manage digital certificates for a contact?

In an open contact window, switch to the Certificates tab.

View all available fields for a contact?

In an open contact window, switch to the All Fields tab. From the "Select from" drop-down list, choose All Contact Fields. All contact-related fields are listed, and you can edit them right here. (You'll be surprised how many you can only get to from here.) You can also use the drop-down list to filter the fields with choices like "Frequently-used fields," "Address fields," and so on.

Create a custom contact field?

In an open contact window, switch to the All Fields tab and click New to open a simple dialog for creating the field. Once created, you can enter values for the field on

the All Fields tab. (You can also add new fields to custom forms, but this book doesn't go into that level of
detail.) Use the Properties button on the All Fields tab to
alter a custom field.

*Create a new contact with the same company information as
an existing contact?*

Select the contact and use Actions → New Contact from
Same Company. A new contact form appears with the
Company name, Business address, and Business phone
fields already filled in.

Create a new contact for someone that sent me an email?

Drag the email message to a contacts folder. A new form
appears with the name and email address filled in. The
text of the message is included in the free-form text field
on the contact form.

In an open email message (or in the Preview pane), right-
click any email address (in the From, To, or Cc fields)
and choose Add to Contacts.

TIP

Drag items to other types of folders (e.g., an email message to a contacts folder) using the right mouse button to
open a pop-up menu at the destination with additional
options for creating the new item.

Display details of a phone number?

Double-click the phone number or click the Edit icon (a
pencil) that appears to the right of an active phone number field.

Have Outlook check for duplicates when I create a new contact?

Outlook checks for duplicate contacts by default when
you create a new contact. If it detects a duplicate (based
on whether it has the same name or email address), Outlook offers to create the duplicate contact or add the new
information to the existing contact.

You can change whether Outlook checks for duplicates using Tools → Options → Contact Options → "Check for duplicate contacts" from the main Outlook window.

Change how a contact is filed?

In an open contact window, use the drop-down list to the right of the "File as" field to choose from one of five preset ways to file the contact (last name first, first name first, just by last name, etc.). This field determines how the contacts are ordered and displayed in the Display pane. You can also type anything you like in this field instead of using the five default methods. For example, you could use a contact's nickname.

Change the default method for how all contacts are filed?

Tools → Options → Contact Options → Default "File As" Order.

Create a new distribution list?

File → New → Distribution List or Ctrl-Shift-L from any folder.

When in a contacts folder, use Actions → New Distribution List or right-click the blank area in the Display pane and choose New Distribution List.

A distribution list (or mailing list) is a container that holds other contacts or email addresses. Sending a message to a distribution list sends the message to all included contacts. In the Distribution List window (Figure 5-2), give the list a name. Click Select Members to choose members from your contacts list. Click Add New to create a member for which no contact exists (by entering a name and email address). Members who are contacts have an icon that looks like a contact card; all other members look like a Rolodex card. Click Update Now to update the members of the list based on any changes you have made to their contact information.

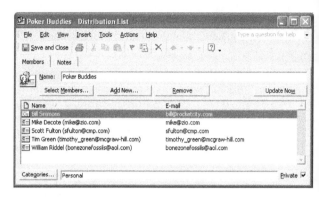

Figure 5-2. Creating a distribution list

Create a new contacts folder?

File → New → Folder. Enter a folder name, select "Contact Items" for its contents, choose where to place the folder, and click OK.

Specify whether a contacts folder is included in the Outlook Address Book?

By default, all new contacts folders are included in the Outlook Address Book. To change this, right-click any contacts folder (including the default Contacts folder) and choose Properties → Outlook Address Book → Show this folder as an e-mail Address Book. You can also enter a name that should appear in the address book to denote the folder (by default, the folder's name is used).

Using Contacts

Find all contacts based on part of a name?

Type part of a name into the Find a Contact box on the Standard toolbar and press Enter.

Create a new email message to a particular contact?

Select the contact (or contacts) and use Actions → New Message to Contact. You can also right-click a contact and select New Message to Contact.

Be sure to read the earlier note about what happens when a contact has multiple email addresses.

Create a meeting request for a contact?

Select the contact and choose Actions → New Meeting Request to Contact.

Right-click the contact and choose New Meeting Request to Contact. This opens a window that is a cross between an email message and an appointment. Fill out the details of the meeting and send the message. An appointment is created in your Calendar, and the recipient can accept or decline the request. See Part IV for more on meeting requests and calendar functions.

Create an appointment for a contact?

Select the contact and choose Actions → New Appointment with Contact.

Right-click the contact and choose New Appointment with Contact.

Create a task for a contact?

Select the contact and choose Actions → New Task for Contact. A new task is created for the associated contact. See Part VI for more on using tasks.

Right-click the contact and choose New Task for Contact.

Use Microsoft Word to create a new letter to a contact?

Select the contact and choose Actions → New Letter to Contact. This starts Microsoft Word and launches the New Letter Wizard, with the contact details already filled in.

Right-click the contact and choose New Letter to Contact.

Use contacts to start a mail merge in Microsoft Word?

Select the contact in Outlook. To select multiple contacts, hold down the Ctrl key and click each contact to
add them to the selection. When the contacts are
selected, use Tools → Mail Merge. Fill in the details of
the merge to create a new merge document in Word.

Make a contact private?

In an open contact window, select the Private option.
This is useful if you use a shared contacts folder.

Dial a contact's phone number?

Right-click the contact and choose Call Contact to use
the default phone number.

Select the contact and use the Actions → Call Contact
submenu to choose from all available phone numbers for
the contact.

In an open contact window, use Actions → Call Contact
or the AutoDialer button on the Standard toolbar.

From anywhere in Outlook, press Ctrl-Shift-D and
choose a contact from the drop-down list.

Call someone who is not in the contacts list?

When viewing any contacts folder, use Actions → Call
Contact → New Call (or press Ctrl-Shift-D from any
folder). Enter the phone number and click Start Call.

Add a speed-dial entry?

> When viewing any contacts folder, use Actions → Call Contact → New Call (or press Ctrl-Shift-D from any folder). On the New Call dialog, click Dialing Options. On the Dialing Options dialog that opens (Figure 5-3), enter a name and phone number and click Add to add it to the speed-dial list. If you enter a name that is close to an existing contact's name, Outlook will fill in the phone number for you.

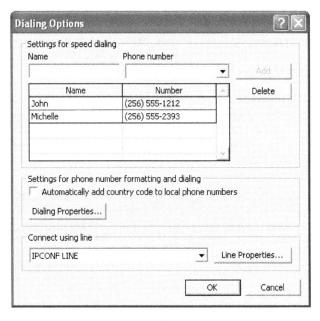

Figure 5-3. Setting up a speed-dial list

Remove a speed-dial entry?

> Open the speed-dial dialog (Figure 5-3), select the entry, and click Delete.

Dial a speed-dial entry?

> From any contacts folder or an open contacts window, use the Actions → Call Contact → Speed Dial submenu to select an entry.

Connect to a contact using NetMeeting?

> Select the contact and choose Actions → Call Using Net-Meeting.
>
> Right-click the contact and choose Call Using NetMeeting.

NOTE

For this command to work, you must set up the contact's NetMeeting information. Use the Details tab of an open contact window to do this.

Flag a contact for follow-up?

> Select a contact or open a contact window and use Actions → Follow Up or Ctrl-Shift-G. You can also right-click a contact and choose Follow Up. The Flag for Follow Up dialog is shown in Figure 5-4.

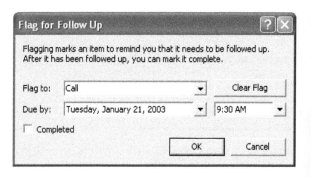

Figure 5-4. Flagging a contact to follow up with later

> Flagging marks a contact to remind you of something. From the "Flag to" drop-down, you can choose remind-

---

ers such as Call, Arrange Meeting, or Send E-Mail. Optionally, you can set a due date and time. If you set a time, Outlook will pop up a reminder for you at that time. Flagged items are indicated in both card and table views in the main Outlook window.

Send a contact's information as a vCard?

Select the contact (or open a contact window) and use Actions → Forward as vCard.

NOTE

The vCard standard is supported by many email clients and allows contact information to be exchanged easily. The vCard is attached to an email message and includes most of the information in the contact file.

Automatically include a vCard with my information with outgoing messages?

Tools → Options → Mail Format → Signatures. Create a new email signature or edit an existing one (see Part III for more on signatures). On the Edit Signature dialog, use the vCard options section to pick an existing vCard or create a new one from a contact.

Create a vCard from a contact?

Open a contact window and choose File → Export to vCard file. Choose a location to save the vCard. You can then include the vCard as an attachment in email messages. You can also open and edit it right from Windows.

Use a vCard someone else sends me?

If you receive a vCard (usually as an attachment to an email message), just drag it to a contacts folder to create a contact from it. You can also open it or save it to a Windows folder like any other attachment.

View a map for a contact's address?

Open the contact's window and use Actions → Display Map of Address (or click the Map button on the Standard toolbar). This opens the MSN Maps & Directories web site and automatically performs a search on the contact's address.

Linking Contacts with Other Items

Link a contact to an existing Outlook item?

Select a contact (or open a contact's window) and choose Actions → Link → Items. The dialog that opens lets you browse through Outlook folders, select items, and link them to the contact.

Open the existing Outlook item and use the Contacts button to pick the contacts to link with it.

NOTE

You can only link contacts to items located in the same *.pst* file as the contact. This means that if you store items in other *.pst* files or use Outlook's AutoArchive (which moves items to an *archive.pst* file), you won't be able to link to those items. Existing links to items that are moved to another *.pst* file are broken.

Link a contact to a new Outlook item?

Whenever you create a new item (including a contact), you can link it to contacts using the Contacts button in the item's window. The one exception is notes. To link a note, you must click the control button in the upper-left corner of an open note window and choose Contacts.

Link a contact to a document?

Select a contact (or open its window) and choose Actions → Link → File. This creates a journal entry that links the contact to the file.

Use links I've created to contacts?

Open a contact's window and switch to the Activities tab. By default, all items linked to the contact are displayed.

This can take a few minutes while Outlook searches for items, but you can click Stop at any time to stop the search. Choose an option from the Show drop-down list to specify the items you want to see (E-Mail, Journal entries, and so on). Note that unless you have specifically linked items to the contact, the only types of items that show up on this tab are email messages containing the contact's primary email address in one of the headers. Double-click any item in the list to open and use it.

Remove a link to an item from a contact?

Open the item that contains the link to the contact. You can do this by finding the item in Outlook and opening it or by opening it from the contact's Activities tab. Remove the contact from the item's open window.

View journal entries for a contact?

Open the contact, switch to the Activities tab, and select Journal from the Show drop-down list.

Create a journal entry for a contact?

Select the contact (or open the contact's window) and choose Actions → New Journal Entry for Contact.

Right-click the contact and choose New Journal Entry for Contact.

Automatically record journal entries for a contact?

Tools → Options → Journal Options. Select a contact and the activities to record. See Part VIII for more information on using the Journal.

Changing Contact Views

View contacts as address cards?

Select a contacts folder and use View → Current View → Address Cards or Detailed Address Cards. These views are also available from the Current View drop-down list on the Advanced toolbar.

Browse through an address card view?

Address Cards are designed to look something like Rolodex cards (Figure 5-5). Items are sorted according to their File As fields. You can browse through items by using the scrollbars or by clicking the letters to the right of the Display pane. You can also start typing the first few letters of a name and the display will jump there. Double-click any card to open the contact.

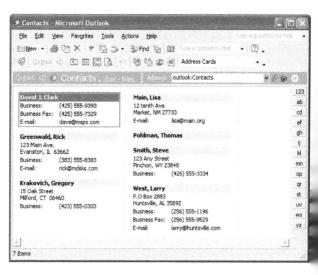

Figure 5-5. Flipping through address cards

Make address cards fit better in the Display pane?

Right-click any open space in the Display pane and choose Best Fit.

Show empty fields in address card views?

Use View → Current View → Customize Current View → Other Settings → Show empty fields.

Right-click any blank space in the view and choose Show Empty Fields.

Allow editing directly in cells of a table or card view?

Use View → Current View → Customize Current View → Other Settings → Allow in-cell editing.

Right-click any blank space in the view and choose Other Settings → Allow in-cell editing.

Remove a field from the contact card view?

Use View → Current View → Customize Current View → Fields (or right-click a blank space in the view and choose Fields). Remove items from the "Show these fields in this order" box.

Change the width of contact cards?

Use View → Current View → Customize Current View → Other Settings → Card width.

Right-click any blank space in the view and choose Other Settings → Card width.

Change the height of the address field in contact card views?

Use View → Current View → Customize Current View → Other Settings → Multi-line field height. Set the value to 3 so you can type a full address directly into the card.

Right-click any blank space in the view and choose Other Settings → Multi-line field height.

View contacts in table views?

Select a contacts folder and use the View → Current View submenu. The Phone List view presents a simple table of contact names and phone numbers. The other table views (all starting with "By") let you sort the contacts by category, location, and so on. These views are also available from the Current View drop-down list on the Advanced toolbar.

Show a "new item" row in a table view?

Use View → Current View → Customize Current View → Other Settings → Show "new item" row. This row appears at the top of the table. Click it to create a new contact.

Right-click any blank space in the view and choose Other Settings → Show "new item" row.

Configure fonts used in any view?

Use View → Current View → Customize Current View → Other Settings.

Right-click any blank space in the view and choose Other Settings.

Change the grid lines used in a table view?

Use View → Current View → Customize Current View → Other Settings. You can also right-click any blank space in the view and choose Other Settings. Use options in the Grid lines section to choose a style (including no lines at all), a line color, and whether group headings should be shaded.

This part of the book provides quick answers about managing Outlook tasks and is divided into the following three categories:

- Creating and managing tasks
- Delegating tasks
- Viewing tasks

Within these categories, tasks are presented as answers to "How do I..." questions (e.g., "How do I assign priorities to tasks?"), followed by concise instructions for completing the task.

Creating and Managing Tasks

Create a task?

Switch to a task folder and click the New Task button on the Standard toolbar or choose File → New → Task.

Double-click any blank area in the Display pane of a task folder. You can also right-click the area and choose New Task.

In most table views, a blank field labeled "Click here to add a new task" appears at the top of the list. Click it and start typing.

Create a new task in the default Tasks folder without leaving the folder I'm in?

Select File → New → Task regardless of which folder you're viewing. You can also click the down arrow next to the New button on the Standard toolbar.

Open an existing task?

Double-click the task.

Select the task. Use File → Open → Selected Items, press the Enter key, or press Ctrl-O.

Right-click the task and choose Open.

Delete a task?

Select one or more tasks. Choose Edit → Delete, press Ctrl-D, or press the Delete key.

Right-click any task or selected group of notes and choose Delete.

Drag a task or selected group of tasks to the Deleted Items folder.

TIP

Hold the Shift key while deleting a task using any of these methods (except Ctrl-D) to delete the task permanently instead of moving it to the Deleted Items folder.

Print a task?

Select a task (or group of tasks). Choose File → Print, press Ctrl-P, press the Print button on the Standard toolbar, or right-click the task and choose Print.

Set the due date for a task?

In an open task window, enter a date in the Due Date box.

For a closed task in any table view, enter a date in the Due Date column.

Set a start date for a task?

In an open task window, enter a date in the Start Date box. A task may have a due date without having a star date, but it may not have a start date without having a due date.

TIP

If you often use start dates for tasks, right-click the column headers of any table view, select Field Chooser, and drag the Start Date field into position on the header.

Set or adjust a reminder for a task?
   Open the task. Select or clear the Reminder option. Use the date and time fields to specify when an alert should open.

Change the default reminder time for new tasks?
   Tools → Options → Reminder time.

Change whether reminders are automatically set for tasks with due dates?
   In Outlook 2002, Tools → Options → Preferences → Task Options → Set reminders on tasks with due dates.

   In Outlook 2000, Tools → Options → Other → Advanced Options → Advanced Tasks → Set reminders on tasks with due dates.

Change or disable the reminder sound for a task?

Open the task and click the Reminder Sound button (its icon looks like a speaker). Clear the "Play this sound" checkbox to disable sound (the reminder still happens). Click Browse to find a new *.wav* file to use for the sound. Changing the sound in this manner affects only the open task.

Change or disable the default reminder sound?
   Tools → Options → Other → Advanced Options → Reminder Options.

Assign priorities to tasks?
   Open the task and use the Priority drop-down list on the Task tab to choose High, Normal, or Low. Priorities are used for grouping tasks.

In many table views, assign a priority by clicking the priority column (labeled with an exclamation point). Add this column to any table view by right-clicking the column header and clicking Field Chooser.

Sort tasks according to priority?

In any table view, click the Priority column header (the exclamation point) to sort tasks by priority. Click it again to reverse the sort order.

Rename a task?

Open the task and change the Subject box.

In any table view, click the task name to change it.

Make a task private?

Open the task and click the Private checkbox (at the lower-right of the task box). This is useful for hiding tasks (and other items) from people when you share a tasks folder.

Change the status of a task?

Open the task and choose an option from the Status drop-down list. Options include Not Started, In Progress, Completed, Waiting on Someone Else, and Deferred.

In the Detailed List view, click the status column of any task to access the same options. In other table views, right-click any column header and use the Field Chooser to add this column.

Track completion of a task?

Open the task and enter a number in the % Complete field.

This field is also available in the Detailed List view. To add it to other table views, use the Field Chooser.

Mark a task complete?

Open the task and either set its status to Completed or set the % Complete field to 100. You can also change these values in many table fields.

In the Simple List view, click the checkbox in the Complete column to mark a task as complete. You can add this column to any view using the Field Chooser.

Change the color of overdue tasks in table views?

Tools → Options → Preferences → Task Options → Overdue task color. The default setting is red.

Change the color of completed tasks in table views?

Tools → Options → Preferences → Task Options → Completed task color. The default setting is grey.

Record time spent on a task?

Open a task and switch to the Details tab. Use the Total Work and Actual Work fields to enter time values. Total Work is meant to be an estimate of the total number of hours a task will take to complete. Actual Work represents the actual number of hours you have put into a task. Filling in these fields is completely up to you, but this option might take on more importance if Outlook is set up to synchronize with planning software such as Microsoft Project. Use the Field Chooser to add these fields to table views.

NOTE

Outlook 2000 automatically changes the entries in the Total Work and Actual Work fields depending on the number you enter. Entering "40 hours", for example, changes the field to read "1 week", and "22 hours" becomes "2.75 days". You can change which numbers are affected by using the two "Task working hours" options on Tools → Options → Other → Advanced Options. In Outlook 2002, these fields stay as you type them. Though the "Task working hours" options are still available in 2002, they don't seem to do much.

Record mileage traveled in association with a task?

Open a task, switch to the Details tab, and use the Mileage field. Use the Field Chooser to add this field to table views.

Assign a contact to a task?

> In an open task window, click Contacts to open a dialog for associating contacts.

Assign a category to a task?

> Select a task and choose Edit → Categories.
>
> Right-click a task and choose Categories.
>
> Open a task and use the Categories button.

Create a recurring task?

> In any open task window, click the Recurrence button on the Standard toolbar to open the Task Recurrence dialog (Figure 6-1). Choose how often the task should appear—Daily, Weekly, Monthly, or Yearly—and then set the recurrence schedule (such as Weekly every Monday and Thursday). The task is given a due date of the first date of the recurrence schedule. When you mark the task complete, a new task (actually a copy) appears with its due date set at the next recurrence. You can also have a task automatically regenerate a set amount of time (such as 3 days) after the current task is marked complete.

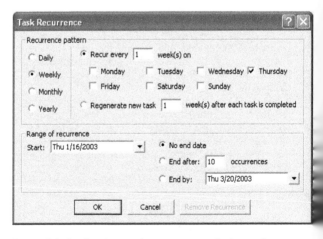

Figure 6-1. Configuring a task to recur at regular intervals

Stop a recurring task?
> In any open task window, click the Recurrence button on the Standard toolbar and then click Remove Recurrence.

Skip an occurrence of a recurring task?
> Open the task and in the task window, choose Actions → Skip Occurrence.

Delegating Tasks

Create a task request?
> From any folder, File → New → Task Request or Ctrl-Shift-U.

> From any tasks folder, use Actions → New Task Request, or right-click any blank space in the view and choose New Task Request.

NOTE

Assigning tasks can be tricky, especially in Outlook 2000. Ideally, both the assigner and assignee should be using the same version of Outlook and should send tasks using HTML-formatted messages. If you vary from this scheme (by using different versions of Outlook, using RTF messages, or whatever), you may have to do some tinkering to get it to work.

Assign an existing task to someone else?
> Right-click the task and choose Assign Task. Enter the email address, configure the task options, and click Send.

Accept or decline a task request?
> Open the task request or right-click the request. Click Accept or Decline. These options are also available in the Preview pane. Whether you accept or decline, you are given the chance to edit your response. If you accept, a copy of the accepted task goes to your Tasks folder.

Reclaim ownership of a declined task?
    Open the message declining the task and click the Return to Task List button.

Send a comment about an assigned task?
    Right-click the task and choose Reply (or Reply to All). Comments are sent as regular email messages.

    In an open task window, choose Actions → Reply (or Reply to All).

Send a status report for a task?
    Open the task and choose Actions → Send Status Report in the task window. Status reports automatically update the owner's copy of the task when opened.

Specify whether status reports are automatically sent when tasks I've assigned are completed?
    In Outlook 2002, Tools → Options → Preferences → Task Options → Send status reports when assigned tasks are completed.

    In Outlook 2000, Tools → Options → Other → Advanced Options → Advanced Tasks → Send status reports when assigned tasks are completed.

Automatically keep copies of tasks I assign?
    In Outlook 2002, Tools → Options → Preferences → Task Options → Keep updated copies of assigned tasks on my task list.

    In Outlook 2000, Tools → Options → Other → Advanced Options → Advanced Tasks → Keep updated copies of assigned tasks on my task list.

Forward a task to others without assigning it to them?
    Select the task. Use Actions → Forward or press Ctrl-F.

    Right-click the task and choose Forward.

Viewing Tasks

Change the order of tasks in a table view?

In most table views, you can drag tasks higher or lower on the list if the view has no sort order, grouping, or filter applied to it. The Simple List and Detailed List views are two examples. Once the tasks are in the order you want, select Actions → Save Task Order to keep them that way—again, assuming you don't apply any custom filters, groupings, or sorts.

View a list of all tasks?

View → Current View → Simple List provides a simple table of all tasks that includes only the subject, the due date, and checkboxes for marking tasks as complete.

View → Current View → Detailed List provides a table of all tasks with more fields displayed.

In both of these views, overdue tasks are red and completed tasks are grey by default.

View only completed tasks?

View View → Current View → Completed Tasks or use the Current View drop-down list on the Advanced toolbar.

View only Active tasks?

View → Current View → Active Tasks.

View only Overdue tasks?

View → Current View → Overdue Tasks.

View tasks I have assigned to someone else?

View → Current View → Assignment.

View tasks according to the tasks' owners?

View → Current View → By Person Responsible.

Notes Tasks

This part covers the tasks associated with Outlook's Notes feature. Tasks are presented as answers to "How do I..." questions (e.g., "How do I assign categories to a note?"), followed by concise instructions for completing the task.

Create a note?

Switch to a notes folder and click the New Note button on the Standard toolbar, or choose File → New → Note.

Double-click any blank area in the Display pane of a notes folder to start a new note. You can also right-click the area and choose New Note.

Create a new note in the default Notes folder without leaving the folder I'm in?

Select File → New → Note regardless of which folder you're viewing. You can also click the down arrow next to the New button on the Standard toolbar.

Open an existing note?

Double-click the note.

Select the note. Use File → Open → Selected Items, press the Enter key, or press Ctrl-O.

Right-click the note and choose Open.

Edit a note?

Type text directly into the note window. Select text, and then click the note icon at the top left of the note window to open a command menu with available editing commands. Ctrl-X (cut), Ctrl-C (copy), and Ctrl-V (paste) also work normally (Figure 7-1).

Figure 7-1. The note window and command menu

Note windows do not have scrollbars. Use the down arrow to scroll through the window. Use the drag handle at the bottom right to resize the window.

Save a note?

Notes are saved automatically when you close a note window, as long as you have typed something. Closing an empty window cancels the note. Open notes are also saved automatically every few minutes.

Delete a note?

Select one or more notes. Choose Edit → Delete, press Ctrl-D, or press the Delete key.

Right-click any note or selected group of notes and choose Delete.

Drag a note or selected group of notes to the Deleted Items folder.

Control the name of the note in the Outlook window?

The first line of text in a note serves as the name of the note in the Outlook window. Use names that are short, descriptive, and unique so that you can see the whole name, find a note when you need to, and tell notes apart.

Print a note?
Select a note (or group of notes). Choose File → Print, press Ctrl-P, press the Print button on the Standard toolbar, or right-click the note and choose Print.

Assign categories to a note?
Select a note and choose Edit → Categories.

Right-click a note and choose Categories.

Change the color of a note?
If the note is open, click the icon at the upper-left to open the command menu and select a color from the Color submenu.

Right-click a note that is not open and choose a color from the Color submenu.

When viewing notes by color, drag a note into another color section to change its color.

Change the default color of all new notes?
Tools → Options → Note Options → Color.

Change the default size used for notes?
Tools → Options → Note Options → Size.

Change the font used for notes?
Tools → Options → Note Options → Font. Choose a font, style, size, and color. This setting affects the view of all notes, not just new notes.

Preview a note when I select it in the main view?
> View → Preview Pane (or use the Preview Pane button on the Advanced toolbar).

Show or hide the date and time on note windows?
> Tools → Options → Other → Advanced Options → When viewing Notes, show time and date.

Create a new folder for notes?
> File → New → Folder. Name the folder, select Note Items for the folder's contents, and choose a location.

Send a note via email?
> Select the note. Use Actions → Forward or Ctrl-F. You can also right-click the note and choose Forward. The note is attached to a new email message.

Use a note I receive via email?
> Treat it like any note. Double-click to open it, drag it to a notes folder or the desktop to save it, or drag it to another folder type to create a new item based on the note.

View notes according to their color?
> View → Current View → By Color, or choose By Color from the Current View drop-down menu on the Advanced toolbar.

View notes as icons?
> View → Current View → Icons, or choose Icons from the Current View drop-down menu on the Advanced toolbar. Commands on the Edit menu and buttons on the Standard toolbar let you view large, small, or list icons.

Customize the icon view?
> View → Current View → Customize Current View → Other Settings.
>
> Right-click any blank area of the Display pane and choose Other Settings.

View notes according to their category?

> View → Current View → By Category, or choose By Category from the Current View drop-down menu on the Advanced toolbar.

View a simple list of notes?

> View → Current View → Notes List, or choose Notes List from the Current View drop-down menu on the Advanced toolbar.

Copy a note to my Windows desktop?

> Drag an open note to the desktop to view it there. The note closes when you close Outlook.
>
> Drag a closed note to the desktop to copy it there. You can open and edit the note even when Outlook is closed. The icon remains on the desktop, and you can manipulate it just like any other file. External Outlook items saved in the filesystem use a *.msg* file extension. You can also drag external items back into an Outlook folder.

> Use the right mouse button to drag a note to the desktop. A pop-up menu lets you choose whether to copy or move the note to the desktop.

Minimize or maximize a note window?

> Right-click anywhere on a note's title bar (except on the Close button) to access a menu with window controls. You can also right-click the Windows taskbar button for the note to get the same menu.

Save a note in another format?

> In an open note window, click the upper-left icon to open the command menu and choose Save As.

Associate contacts with a note?

> In an open note window, click the upper-left icon to open the command menu and choose Contacts. A dialog opens for associating contacts. Use the Contacts button to choose contacts from your list.

NOTE

Although you can type contact names directly into the Contacts for Note dialog, you must type them exactly or Outlook will not resolve them correctly. For this reason, it's always better to browse the list.

Create an email message using the text of a note as the message body?

Drag a closed note to any message-type folder (such as the Inbox or Outbox) to create a new email message. The text of the note is automatically entered into the message body.

Create a task, appointment, or contact from a note?

Drag a closed note to any of these types of folders to create a new item of the specified type. For all item types, the note text is entered into the item form. For appointments and tasks, the first line of note text is entered as the subject.

TIP

Drag items to other folders using the right instead of left mouse button for more control. For example, right-dragging a note pops up a menu that lets you choose to move or copy the note, include its text, create a shortcut to the note, or use the note as an attachment.

PART VIII

Journal Tasks

Outlook's Journal provides a way to record activities in your daily routine. These activities might occur within Outlook (such as receiving an email from a particular contact) or outside Outlook (such as recording a journal entry every time you open a Word document). You can even record entries for activities that have nothing to do with your computer (e.g., you can record phone calls or deliveries). Many of these activities (like email) can be set up to create automatic journal entries. For other activities, you'll have to create the entry yourself.

This section of the book covers solutions for using the Journal feature. Within these categories, tasks are presented as answers to "How do I..." questions (e.g., "How do I view journal entries associated with a contact?"), followed by concise instructions for completing the task.

Turn on the journaling feature?

The first time you click the default Journal folder, a dialog asks you whether to turn on automatic journaling. Once you turn it on, automatic journaling stays on (though nothing is automatically recorded until you set it up). The first time you turn on automatic journaling, you are shown the Journal Options dialog (see Figure 8-1). You can get to this dialog later using Tools → Options → Journal Options.

If you tell Outlook not to turn on journaling, it will ask you again each time you return to the folder, unless you select the option "Please do not show me this dialog again" and click No. If you have done this in the past and now want to turn on journaling, use Tools → Options → Journal Options. Outlook prompts you with the dialog once more before giving you access to the Journal Options dialog.

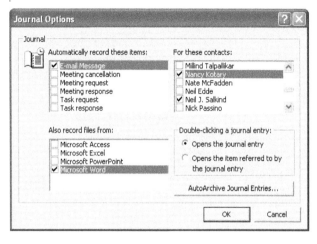

Figure 8-1. Setting automatic journal options

Automatically record email messages to and from certain contacts?

Tools → Options → Journal Options. In the "Automatically record these items" section, select E-mail Message. In the "For these contacts" section, check the contacts to record messages. All messages to and from these contacts are subsequently journaled.

Automatically record meeting requests, responses, or cancellations for certain contacts?

Tools → Options → Journal Options. In the "Automatically record these items" section, select any of the Meeting options, and then select the contacts for whom you want to record journal entries.

Automatically record task requests or responses for certain contacts?

Tools → Options → Journal Options. In the "Automatically record these items" section, select either of the Task options, and then select the contacts for whom you want to record journal entries.

Automatically record when certain types of Office documents are used?

Tools → Options → Journal Options. In the "Also record files from" section, check the programs for which you want to track files. Only Microsoft Office applications are available.

WARNING

Automatically tracking document types can quickly consume system resources and slow down certain tasks. In fact, it often takes documents a full minute longer to close while the journal entries are created. Use file tracking sparingly, or just create manual entries for specific files when the need arises.

Turn off automatic recording of journal entries?

You can stop automatic recording by going to Tools → Options → Journal Options and disabling all options in the "Automatically record these items" and "Also record files from" sections.

NOTE

Once turned on, you can't completely disable automatic journaling. The most you can do is disable the journaling actions in Outlook. A small piece of Outlook code continues to run in the background at all times. However, this code is small enough that it doesn't consume a lot of resources and innocuous enough that it won't really do anything if you have disabled individual journaling actions.

Create a manual journal entry?

Select a journal folder. Use Action → New Entry or Ctrl-N. You can also double-click the blank area in the Display pane when viewing a journal folder.

Use File → New → Journal Entry (or click the down arrow next to the new button on the Standard toolbar and click Journal Entry) to create an entry in the default Journal folder from anywhere in Outlook.

No matter which method you use, you get a blank Journal Entry form (Figure 8-2). Enter a subject and choose an entry type to identify the entry (Phone call, Letter, Meeting, etc.). As with other forms, you can enter a company name, fill in free-form text, and associate contacts and categories. Start time shows the date and time the entry is created (though you can change them). Start Timer and Pause Timer track time spent on the item. The total duration is shown in the Duration field. (You can also use this field to specify a duration instead of using the timer.) Note that the times when you pause and restart the timer are not recorded—only the full duration. You must record additional stop and start times by hand if you need them.

Associate an Outlook item with a manual journal entry?

In an open entry window, use Insert → Item. Choose one or more items from any Outlook folder. Specify if you want to insert the item as text-only (which copies the free-form text field from the item to the field in the journal entry), copy the item as an attachment inside the entry, or create a shortcut to the item.

Create a manual journal entry for a file outside Outlook?

There are several ways to approach this, all aimed at associating a document with a journal entry and optionally tracking the time spent on it.

The easiest method is to find the file in Windows Explorer and then right-drag it onto a journal folder. This pops up a menu where you can choose to create a

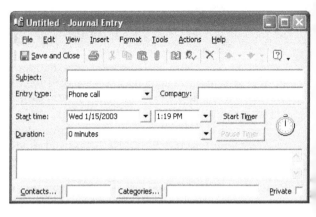

Figure 8-2. Creating a manual journal entry

journal entry with a shortcut to the document inside or create an entry with an actual copy of the document. I favor using shortcuts and leaving the original document where it is. If you copy the document, it is stored inside your *.pst* file, is accessible only through Outlook, and is not updated automatically if you change the copy stored in its original location.

You can also insert a document into an existing journal entry. If you want a copy of the document, just drag the file from Windows Explorer into an open journal entry window. Another way to do this is to choose Insert → File and browse for the document.

Choose Insert → Object for even more control (Figure 8-3). The Create New option lets you pick from a number of file types and create a blank document attached to the entry. The Create from File option lets you browse for a file. The file is copied as an attachment unless you select the Link option, in which case a shortcut is created.

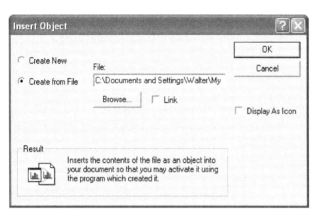

Figure 8-3. Inserting an object into a journal entry

Open a Journal entry?

Double-click the entry.

Select the entry. Use File → Open → Selected Items, press the Enter key, or press Ctrl-O.

Right-click the entry and choose Open.

Change whether double-clicking an entry opens the entry or the item it is associated with?

Tools → Options → Journal Options. Choose the desired option from the "Double-clicking a journal entry" section.

Delete a journal entry?

Select one or more entries. Choose Edit → Delete, press Ctrl-D, or press the Delete key.

Right-click any entry or selected group of entries and choose Delete.

Drag a note or selected group of entries to the Deleted Items folder.

TIP

Hold the Shift key while deleting an entry using any of the deletion methods (except Ctrl-D) to delete the note permanently instead of moving it to the Deleted Items folder.

Save a journal entry as another file type?

In an open entry window or with a closed entry selected, use File → Save As.

Print a journal entry?

Right-click the entry and choose Print.

In an open entry window, choose File → Print or press Ctrl-P.

Print entries in a view?

You cannot print a timeline view. For other views, select the entries to print and use File → Print or Ctrl-P.

Associate contacts with a journal entry?

In an open entry window, click Contacts to open a dialog for associating contacts.

View journal entries associated with a contact?

Open the contact, switch to the Activities tab, and choose Journal on the Show drop-down list.

Record the date and time I worked with a contact?

Select the contact and choose Action → New Journal Entry for Contact.

Right-click the contact and choose New Journal Entry for Contact.

Change the date of a journal entry so it appears in a different place on the timeline?

Open the journal entry and enter a new date and time.

Change how entries are listed in the timeline view?

Three of the journal views are timeline views: By Contact, By Category, and By Type (meaning type of journal entry). Each of these views groups items on the timeline according to the selection. Figure 8-4 shows a timeline view grouped by contact.

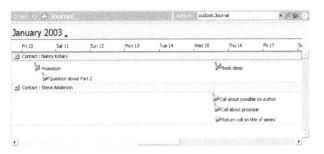

Figure 8-4. Grouping a timeline view by contact

Show week numbers in the heading for the timeline view?

View → Current View → Customize Current View → Other Settings → Show week numbers.

Right-click the blank space in a timeline view and select Other Settings → Show week numbers.

Adjust the size of the text labels shown for entries in a timeline view?

View → Current View → Customize Current View → Other Settings (or right-click the blank space and choose Other Settings) and set "Maximum label width" to the number of characters you would like. You can also specify whether labels are shown in month views.

Change the start and end times used to display journal entries in a timeline view?

View → Current View → Customize Current View → Fields.

View journal entries in a table?

There are three table-style views predefined for journal folders: Entry List (shows all entries), Last Seven Days (filters out entries older than one week), and Phone Calls (shows only entries of the Phone Call type). These are all available on the View → Current View menu and on the Current View drop-down list on the Advanced toolbar.

Create a new journal folder?

File → New → Folder. Name the folder, select Journal Items for the folder's contents, and choose a location.

Send a journal entry via email?

Select the entry. Use Actions → Forward or Ctrl-F. You can also right-click the entry and choose Forward. The entry is attached to a new email message.

Use a journal entry I receive via email?

Treat it like any entry. Double-click to open it, drag it to a journal folder or the desktop to save it, or drag it to another folder type to create a new item based on the entry.

Copy or move a journal entry to the Windows desktop?

Drag a closed entry to the desktop to copy it there. You can open and edit the entry even when Outlook is closed. The icon remains on the desktop, and you can manipulate it just like any file. External Outlook items saved in the filesystem use a *.msg* file extension. You can also drag external items back into an Outlook folder.

Use the right mouse button to drag a note to the desktop. A pop-up menu lets you choose whether to copy or move the note to the desktop.

Create an email message using the text of an entry as the message body?

Drag a closed entry to any message-type folder (such as the Inbox or Outbox) to create a new message. The text of the entry is automatically entered into the message body.

Create a task, appointment, or contact from an entry?

Drag a closed entry to any of these types of folders to create a new item of the specified type. For all item types, the entry text is entered into the item form.

TIP

Drag items to other folders using the right instead of left mouse button to open a menu with options to move or copy the entry, include its text, create a shortcut to the entry, or use the entry as an attachment.

PART IX

Outlook Reference

This part of the book contains many tables of information that is otherwise difficult to find. Specifically, tables in this part cover:

- Useful commands that are not included on any toolbar or menu by default
- Locations of important Outlook files and default paths for saving files
- Predefined views and print styles
- Internet headers that may appear in a message
- Switches used to start Outlook from the command line
- Default key combinations (keyboard shortcuts)

Command Reference

There are hundreds of commands available in Outlook, but only some of them have made their way onto Outlook's menus and toolbars or have keyboard shortcuts. Table 9-1 lists some useful commands and suggestions on where you might add them. These commands are found in the Tools → Customize → Commands dialog—in this dialog, you can add your chosen commands to customize your menus and toolbars. The commands are listed by category and command (e.g., View → News means the News command in the View category). Check out "Customizing Menus and Tool bars" in Part II for details on adding these commands to the interface.

Table 9-1. Useful Outlook commands

Command	Action	Suggested uses
View → News	Opens the default newsreader configured on the computer. You can also use the menu command View → Go To → News.	Add a button to a toolbar or menu for quick access.
View → Other Settings	The same as using the menu command View → Current View → Customize Current View → Other Settings.	Add to a toolbar if you change column and row settings on views often.
Tools → Run Rules Now	Opens the dialog for running rules, the same as using the menu command Tools → Rules Wizard → Run Now.	Add to a toolbar to quickly run rules when Outlook "forgets" to apply them to incoming mail.
Actions → Plain Text Actions → Rich Text Actions → Microsoft Word (Plain Text) Actions → HTML (No Stationery)	Each of these starts a new message using the specified format. These are also available using the Actions → New Mail Message Using submenu and are useful if you need to send messages in different formats.	Add buttons to a toolbar for quickly creating messages of a specified format.
Actions → Add to Junk Senders List Actions → Add to Adult Content Senders List	Add the sender of a selected email message to the indicated junk filtering list. Also available using the Actions → Junk E-mail submenu.	Add toolbar buttons for managing Outlook's junk mail tool.
Actions → Post Reply to Folder	Opens a post form with the body of the selected email message quoted in the body of the post. Useful for leaving a note in a folder about a particular message.	Add to a toolbar or menu.

Table 9-1. Useful Outlook commands (continued)

Command	Action	Suggested uses
New Menu	Creates a new menu on the menu bar or a toolbar that you can use to store custom commands, seldom-used commands, or just organize commands the way you want.	Add to a toolbar or menu.

Important File Locations

Table 9-2 lists the locations of Outlook's important files and folders. To perform a full backup of your data store and settings, you'll need to back up the items in all of these locations. Since some of these locations are user-definable (like the *.pst* file), this list represents only the default locations.

Table 9-2. Default file locations

File or location	Extension	Path	User-definable?
Information Stores	.pst	\Application Data\Microsoft\Outlook	Yes
Offline Stores	.ost	\Local Settings\Application Data\Microsoft\Outlook	Yes
Menu and View Settings	.dat	\Application Data\Microsoft\Outlook	No
Outlook Bar Shortcuts	.fav	\Application Data\Microsoft\Outlook	No
Default Program Settings	.inf	\Application Data\Microsoft\Outlook	No
Outlook Nicknames (user mail settings)	.nick	\Application Data\Microsoft\Outlook	No
Rules	.rwz	\Application Data\Microsoft\Outlook	No
Print Styles	None	\Application Data\Microsoft\Outlook	No
Signatures	.rtf, .txt, .html	\Application Data\Microsoft\Signatures	No

Table 9-2. Default file locations (continued)

File or location	Extension	Path	User-definable?
Stationery	.html	\Application Data\Microsoft\Stationary	No
Custom Forms	None	\Local Settings\Application Data\Microsoft\Forms	Customized default forms, no; new forms, yes.
Dictionary	.txt	\Application Data\Microsoft\Proof	No
Templates	.oft	\Application Data\Microsoft\Templates	No

There are two main folders in which items are stored: \Application Data and \Local Settings\Application Data. On Windows 2000/XP, these folders are located in the \Documents and Settings\<username> folder (e.g., mine is \Documents and Settings\walter\Application Data). On Windows NT 4.0, they are stored in the \WINNT\Profiles\<username> folder. On Windows 9x/Me, these folders are stored in the \Windows folder.

Views and Print Styles

Each major folder type in Outlook (email, calendar, contacts, tasks, notes, and journal) has a number of available view styles. In a contacts folder, for example, you can view contacts as address cards or in a table. When you print the contents of a folder (for example, when you print a list of contacts), the view style determines how items are printed. Table 9-3 lists the predefined views available for each folder type and the print styles with which these views are associated.

Table 9-3. Outlook's default views and print styles

Folder type	Default view	Print style
Mail	Messages	Table, Memo
	Messages with AutoPreview	Table, Memo

Table 9-3. Outlook's default views and print styles (continued)

Folder type	Default view	Print style
	By Follow Up Flag	Table, Memo
	Last Seven Days	Table, Memo
	Flagged for Next Seven Days	Table, Memo
	By Conversation Topic	Table, Memo
	By Sender	Table, Memo
	Unread Messages	Table, Memo
	Sent To	Table, Memo
	Message Timeline	You can't print a timeline view; you must print individual items
Calendar	Day/Week/Month	Daily
	Day/Week/Month with AutoPreview	Daily
	Active Appointments	Table
	Events	Table
	Annual Events	Table
	Recurring Appointments	Table
	By Category	Table
Contacts	Address Cards	Card
	Detailed Address Cards	Card
	Phone List	Table
	By Category	Table
	By Company	Table
	By Location	Table
	By Follow Up Flag	Table
Tasks	Simple List	Table, Memo
	Detailed List	Table, Memo
	Active Tasks	Table, Memo
	Next Seven Days	Table, Memo
	Overdue Tasks	Table, Memo

Table 9-3. Outlook's default views and print styles (continued)

Folder type	Default view	Print style
	By Category	Table, Memo
	Assignment	Table, Memo
	By Person Responsible	Table, Memo
	Completed Tasks	Table, Memo
	Task Timeline	You can't print a timeline view; you must print individual items
Notes	Icons	N/A
	Notes List	Table, Memo
	Last Seven Days	Table, Memo
	By Category	Table, Memo
	By Color	Table, Memo
Journal	By Type	You can't print a timeline view; you must print individual items
	By Contact	You can't print a timeline view; you must print individual items
	By Category	You can't print a timeline view; you must print individual items
	Entry List	Table, Memo
	Last Seven Days	Table, Memo
	Phone Calls	Table, Memo

Internet Headers

Simple Mail Transfer Protocol (SMTP)—the protocol that delivers mail from your client to mail servers and between mail servers—uses headers to label messages. You are no doubt familiar with basic headers such as To: and From:. Some headers are not shown in Outlook, but you can view them by right-clicking a message and choosing Options. Toward the bottom of the dialog that opens, you'll see a list of Internet headers. Table 9-4 lists the common Internet headers. The first six entries are basic headers displayed in the main Outlook window. To view the rest, you must use the Options command.

Table 9-4. Common Internet headers

Header	Description
Date:	Specifies the date the message was created and sent. If a client does not include a date, a mail server along the way might stamp a date on the message.
To:	Generally contains the addresses of the message recipients . The To: field does not always contain the true recipient's address, especially in the case of mailing lists.
From:	The From line generally indicates who the message is from. Because this information is specified by the client software, it is not always accurate. Any information can be entered in the From: field by the client.
Subject:	A free-form text field indicating the subject of a message.
Cc:	Carbon Copy. Specifies additional recipients of the message, for whom it might be less important than for those in the To: field.
Bcc:	Blind Carbon Copy. Addresses in this field are used to copy someone on a message without the other recipients' knowledge.
Return-Path:	Outlook automatically refers to this header to determine what address to use when replying to a message. This information can be changed in the client software, so it is not always accurate.
Received:	This actually appears as two headers. The first Received: header contains a list of senders who may have handled the message along its way to you. The most recent information is at the top of the list. The second Received: header indicates where the message originated.
Organization:	This field is entered into the client and can appear as anything. If no organization name is entered into the client, the outgoing mail server (i.e., your ISP) will likely stamp its organization's name on the message.
Message-Id:	A long ID stamped on the message by the originating mail server to identify the message and track its status.
X-Sender:	Extra sender information included by some client software to add another layer of authentication.
X-Mailer:	Again, only some client software use this header. It indicates the type and version of client software used to send the message.

Table 9-4. Common Internet headers (continued)

Header	Description
Mime-Version:	Multipurpose Internet Mail Extensions (MIME)–compatible clients use this header to determine what to do with attachment files.
Content-Type:	Tells the receiving client exactly what MIME types are included with a message.

Startup Switches

Like most programs, you can start Outlook from the Windows command line (Start → Programs → MS-DOS Prompt in Windows 95/98/Me and Start → Programs → Accessories → Command Prompt in Windows 2000/XP) or create customized shortcuts for starting Outlook. At the command-line prompt, type *outlook.exe* to launch Outlook normally, or add one of the switches listed in Table 9-5 after this command to affect how Outlook launches.

Table 9-5. Command-line startup switches

Startup Switch	Description
/a path:\<filename>	Opens a new email message with the specified file attached
/c ipm.activity	Opens a Journal entry form
/c ipm.appointment	Opens an Appointment entry form
/c ipm.contact	Opens a Contact entry form
/c ipm.distlist	Creates a new Distribution List
/c ipm.note	Opens a New Message form
/c ipm.post	Opens a Post or Discussion form
/c ipm.stickynote	Opens a Note form
/c ipm.task	Opens a Task entry form
/checkclient	Runs the prompt to make Outlook the default client for email, news, and contacts
/cleanfinders	Removes saved searches from an Exchange Server store
/cleanfreebusy	Cleans and regenerates free/busy information
/cleanprofile	Removes and recreates Outlook's default profile; used when reverting to a previous version of Outlook after removing a more current version

Table 9-5. Command-line startup switches (continued)

Startup Switch	Description
/cleanpst	Starts Outlook with a "clean" (empty) PST (Internet Only mode available only in Outlook 2000)
/cleanreminders	Cleans and regenerates all reminders
/cleanviews	Restores all views to the default
/CleanSchedPlus	Deletes all Schedule+ data (free/busy information, permissions, and *.cal* file) from the server
/f <msgfilename>	Opens <msgfilename>
/folder	Starts Outlook with Outlook Bar and Folder List turned off
/nopreview	Turns off the Preview pane at startup
/p <msgfilename>	Prints a specified message
/profiles	Starts Outlook with a Choose Profile dialog, regardless of options set
/profile <profilename>	Starts Outlook with a specified profile
/importprf <path\.prf filename>	Creates an Outlook profile based on the information in the specified *.prf* file (Outlook 2002 only)
/recycle	Activates an existing Outlook window
/resetfoldernames	Resets the language of the default folders to the language of the Outlook client (Outlook 2002 only)
/resetfolders	Restores missing or damaged system folders to the default delivery location
/resetoutlookbar	Rebuilds the Outlook Bar to the default configuration
/s <filename>	Loads a specified shortcuts (*.fav*) file
/safe	Starts Outlook without any add-ins, preview pane, or toolbar customization

Keyboard Shortcuts

Outlook supports many built-in key combinations. Don't be overwhelmed, though—find those that represent frequent tasks and start with them. Tables 9-6 through 9-25 show default key combinations grouped by function. Each table focuses on a certain topic in Outlook, such as creating items, working with tasks, or accessing help.

Table 9-6. General program keys

Key	Action
Esc	Cancel current operation
F1	Open Help (or Office Assistant if it is turned on)
Shift-F1	Display Screen Tip for selected item, dialog control, or navigation tool
+ (on numeric keypad)	Expand selected group in Folder List
- (on numeric keypad)	Collapse selected group in Folder List
Enter	Activate item (select folder or open item)
F2	Turn on editing in a field
Arrow Keys	Move from item to item
Ctrl-A	Select all
Ctrl-D	Delete item or selected text
Ctrl-Tab or Ctrl-Page Down	Switch to next tab on a form
Ctrl-Shift-Tab or Ctrl-Page Up	Switch to previous tab on a form
Ctrl-Shift-B	Display address book
Ctrl-Shift-D	Start new call
Ctrl-Shift-F	Use Advanced Find
Ctrl-Shift-G	Flag for Follow Up
Ctrl-Shift-H	Create new Office document
Ctrl-Shift-P	Find people (Outlook 2000 only)
Ctrl-, (comma)	Move to previous open item
Ctrl-. (period)	Move to next open item
Ctrl-Shift-Tab or F6	Switch between panes (Folder List, item view, and Preview pane)

Table 9-7. Keyboard shortcuts for creating items

Key	Action
Ctrl-Shift-A	Create an appointment
Ctrl-Shift-C	Create a contact
Ctrl-Shift-E	Create a folder

Table 9-7. Keyboard shortcuts for creating items (continued)

Key	Action
Ctrl-Shift-J	Create a journal entry
Ctrl-Shift-L	Create a distribution list
Ctrl-Shift-M	Create a message
Ctrl-Shift-Q	Create a meeting request
Ctrl-Shift-N	Create a note
Ctrl-Shift-K	Create a task
Ctrl-Shift-S	Post to selected folder
Ctrl-Shift-U	Create a task request

Table 9-8. Mail shortcuts

Key	Action
Ctrl-Q	Mark as read
Ctrl-R	Reply
Ctrl-Shift-R	Reply to All
Ctrl-F	Forward
Shift-F3	Switch case of selected text (MS-RFT format only)
Ctrl-M or F5	Send/Receive (check for new mail)
Ctrl-K	Check names (default editor, not Word)
Ctrl-Shift-I	Switch to Inbox
Ctrl-Shift-O	Switch to Outbox (in main view)
Ctrl-Shift-O	Convert an HTML or RTF message to plain text (with message window open)
Ctrl-Shift-S	Post to a folder

Table 9-9. Menu shortcuts

Key	Action
Ctrl-S or Shift-F12	Save
Alt-S	Save and close (Contact, Calendar, Journal, and Tasks items)
Alt-S	Send (Mail item)
F12	Save As

Table 9-9. Menu shortcuts (continued)

Key	Action
Ctrl-Y	Go to folder
Shift-Ctrl-I	Go to Inbox folder
Ctrl-Shift-S	Post to a folder
Ctrl-P	Print
Ctrl-N	Create a new message
Ctrl-X or Shift-Delete	Cut to the Clipboard
Ctrl-C or Ctrl-Insert	Copy to the Clipboard
Ctrl-Shift-Y	Copy item
Ctrl-V or Shift-Insert	Paste from the Clipboard
Ctrl-Shift-V	Move item
Ctrl-Z or Alt-Backspace	Undo
Ctrl-D	Delete
Ctrl-A	Select all
Shift-F10	Display context menu
Spacebar	Display Outlook control menu (when menu bar is active)
Alt-Spacebar	Display window control menu
Down Arrow	Select next command on menu
Up Arrow	Select previous command on menu
Left Arrow	Select menu to the left
Right Arrow	Select menu to the right
Ctrl-Down Arrow	Display the full menu when adaptive menus are used
Home	Select first command on menu
End	Select last command on menu
F10 or Alt	Activate menu bar
Shift-Ctrl-Tab	Move between toolbars
Ctrl-Shift-F or F3	Advanced Find
F4	Find text (from open item)
Shift-F4	Find next
F5	Refresh

Table 9-9. Menu shortcuts (continued)

Key	Action
F7	Check spelling (open message form)
Alt-O	Display Favorites menu
Alt-C	Close print preview
Alt-C	Accept (Calendar or Task request)
Alt-D	Decline (Calendar or Task request)
Alt	Close menu and submenu (if open)
Esc	Close menu and submenu

Table 9-10. Toolbar shortcuts

Key	Action
F10	Activate menu bar
Ctrl-Tab	Select next toolbar
Ctrl-Shift-Tab	Select previous toolbar
Tab	Select next button or menu
Shift-Tab	Select previous button or menu
Enter	Activate selection (open menu, press button, enter text)
F11	Enter text in Find a Contact box
Up Arrow or Down Arrow, Enter	Select option from drop-down list or menu

Table 9-11. Dialog box shortcuts

Key	Action
Tab	Move to next option or option group
Shift-Tab	Move to previous option or option group
Ctrl-Tab	Move to next tab
Ctrl-Shift-Tab	Move to previous tab
Down Arrow	Move to next item in drop-down list
Up Arrow	Move to previous item in drop-down list
Home	Move to first item in drop-down list
End	Move to last item in drop-down list

Table 9-11. Dialog box shortcuts (continued)

Key	Action
Spacebar	Perform action assigned to button
Spacebar	Select or clear a checkbox
Alt-Down Arrow	Open a drop-down list
Alt-Up Arrow or Esc	Close a drop-down list
Alt-1	In Open and Save dialog boxes, returns to the previous folder viewed
Alt-2	In Open and Save dialog boxes, goes up one folder level
Alt-3	In Open and Save dialog boxes, activates the Search the Web command
Alt-4	In Open and Save dialog boxes, deletes the selected folder or file
Alt-5	In Open and Save dialog boxes, creates a new folder
Alt-6	In Open and Save dialog boxes, activates the Views drop-down list
Alt-7	In Open and Save dialog boxes, activates the Tools menu
Alt-I or F4	In Open and Save dialog boxes, activates the Look In drop-down list

Table 9-12. Formatting shortcuts

Key	Action
Ctrl-B	Make bold
Ctrl-I	Italicize
Ctrl-U	Underline
Ctrl-Shift-L	Add bullets
Ctrl-L	Left align
Ctrl-E	Center
Ctrl-T	Increase indent
Ctrl-Shift-T	Decrease indent
Ctrl-]	Increase font size
Ctrl-[	Decrease font size
Ctrl-Shift-Z or Ctrl-Spacebar	Clear formatting

Table 9-13. General text selection shortcuts

Key	Action
Home	Move to the beginning of text box
End	Move to the end of text box
Left Arrow	Move one character to the left
Right Arrow	Move one character to the right
Shift-Home	Select from insertion point to the beginning
Shift-End	Select from insertion point to the end
Shift-Left Arrow	Select or deselect one character to the left
Shift-Right Arrow	Select or deselect one character to the right
Ctrl-Shift-Left Arrow	Select or deselect one word to the left
Ctrl-Shift-Right Arrow	Select or deselect one word to the right

Table 9-14. Hyperlink shortcuts

Key	Action
Ctrl-left mouse button	Edit a URL within a message
Shift-left mouse button (specify a browser)	Locate Link Browser
Ctrl-K (when Word is the email editor)	Insert a hyperlink

Table 9-15. Table shortcuts

Key	Action
Enter	Open item
Down Arrow	Go to next item
Up Arrow	Go to previous item
Ctrl-Down Arrow or Up Arrow, then Spacebar to select	Select noncontiguous items
Home	Go to first item
End	Go to last item
Page Down	Go to item at bottom of screen

Table 9-15. Table shortcuts (continued)

Key	Action
Page Up	Go to item at top of screen
Shift-Up Arrow	Extend item selection by one
Shift-Down Arrow	Reduce item selection by one
Ctrl-A	Select all items

Table 9-16. Shortcuts for groups in a table

Key	Action
Enter or Right Arrow	Expand group
Enter or Left Arrow	Collapse group
Up Arrow	Select previous group
Down Arrow	Select next group
Home	Select first group
End	Select last group
Right Arrow	Select first item in expanded group

Table 9-17. Card view shortcuts

Key	Action
Down Arrow	Go to next card
Up Arrow	Go to previous card
Home	Go to first card in folder
End	Go to last card in folder
Page Up	Go to first card on current page
Page Down	Go to first card on next page
Right Arrow	Go to closest card in next column
Left Arrow	Go to closest card in previous column
Ctrl-Spacebar	Select or deselect active card
Ctrl-Shift-Down Arrow	Extend selection to next card
Shift-Down Arrow	Extend selection to next card and deselect previous card
Shift-Up Arrow	Extend selection to previous card and deselect subsequent cards

Table 9-17. Card view shortcuts (continued)

Key	Action
Shift-End	Extend selection to last card
Shift-Home	Extend selection to first card
Shift-Page Up	Extend selection to last card on previous page
Shift-Page Down	Extend selection to first card on next page
Ctrl-Shift-Up Arrow	Extend selection to previous card

Table 9-18. General calendar shortcuts

Key	Action
Ctrl-Tab or F6	Move between Calendar, TaskPad, and Folder List
Tab	Select next appointment
Shift-Tab	Select previous appointment
Right Arrow	Go to next day
Left Arrow	Go to previous day
Tab	Move from item to item
Alt-<n>	View <n> days (0 to 10)
Alt-- (Alt-minus)	Switch to weeks
Alt-=	Switch to months
Alt-Right Arrow	Move selected appointment to next day
Alt-Left Arrow	Move selected appointment to previous day
Alt-Down Arrow	Go to same day in next week (Day and Work Week views)
Alt-Up Arrow	Go to same day in previous week (Day and Work Week Views)
Alt-Down Arrow	Move selected item to same day in next week (Month view)
Alt-Up Arrow	Move selected item to same day in previous week (Month view)

Table 9-19. Date navigator shortcuts

Key	Action
Alt-Home	Go to first day of current week
Alt-End	Go to last day of current week
Alt-Up Arrow	Go to same day in previous week

Table 9-19. Date navigator shortcuts (continued)

Key	Action
Alt-Down Arrow	Go to same day in next week
Alt-Page Up	Go to first day of current month
Alt-Page Down	Go to last day of current month

Table 9-20. Calendar day view shortcuts

Key	Action
Home	Select beginning of work day
End	Select end of work day
Up Arrow	Select previous block of time
Down Arrow	Select next block of time
Page Up	Select block of time at top of screen
Page Down	Select block of time at bottom of screen
Shift-Up Arrow	Extend selected time
Shift-Down Arrow	Reduce selected time
Alt-Up Arrow	Move selected appointment back
Alt-Down Arrow	Move selected appointment forward
Alt-Shift-Up Arrow	Move start of selected appointment
Alt-Shift-Down Arrow	Move end of selected appointment

Table 9-21. Timeline shortcuts with an item selected

Key	Action
Enter	Open selected item
Left Arrow	Open previous item
Right Arrow	Open next item
Shift-Left Arrow	Select adjacent previous items
Shift-Right Arrow	Select adjacent subsequent items
Ctrl-Left Arrow-Spacebar	Select nonadjacent previous items
Ctrl-Right Arrow-Spacebar	Select nonadjacent subsequent items

Table 9-21. Timeline shortcuts with an item selected (continued)

Key	Action
Page Up	Display items one screen above
Page Down	Display items one screen below
Home	Select first item
End	Select last item
Ctrl-Home	Display first item without selecting it
Ctrl-End	Display last item without selecting it

Table 9-22. Timeline shortcuts with a group selected

Key	Action
Enter or Right Arrow	Expand group
Enter or Left Arrow	Collapse group
Up Arrow	Select previous group
Down Arrow	Select next group
Home	Select first group
End	Select last group
Right Arrow	Select first onscreen item in expanded group
Left Arrow	Move back one increment of time
Right Arrow	Move forward one increment of time
Tab	Switch from upper to lower time scale; with lower time scale selected, Tab key selects the first onscreen item or first group
Shift-Tab	Switch from lower to upper time scale

Table 9-23. Print preview shortcuts

Key	Action
Ctrl-F2	Open print preview
Alt-P	Print from print preview
Alt-S, then Alt-U	Print preview page setup
Alt-Z	Zoom
Page Down	Display next page
Page Up	Display previous page

Table 9-23. Print preview shortcuts (continued)

Key	Action
Ctrl-Up Arrow or Home	Display first page
Ctrl-Down Arrow or End	Display last page

Table 9-24. Help shortcuts

Key	Action
F1	Get Help from Office Assistant; opens the main Help window if Assistant is turned off
Alt-F6	Activate the Office Assistant balloon
F6	Switch between the Help topic and the Contents, Answer Wizard, and Index tabs in the Help window
Alt-<n>	Select Help Topic <n>
Alt-Down Arrow	See more Help topics
Alt-Up Arrow	See previous Help topics
Esc	Close Office Assistant message
Tab	Switch between Show All and Hide All at the top of a topic page
Shift-F1	Context sensitive help
Alt-N	Display next tip (when screen tips activated)
Alt-B	Display previous tip
Alt-O	Display the Options menu in a Help window
Ctrl-P	Print the current help topic
Esc	Close tips

Table 9-25. VBA shortcuts

Key	Action
Alt-F8	Open Macro Selector
Alt F-11	Open VBA Development Environment

PART X

Outlook Resources

Internet Sites

Microsoft's Official Outlook Site
Official news and articles with tips and tricks.

http://www.microsoft.com/outlook

Office Update
Microsoft's update site for all versions of Office. It includes service packs and patches, and a download center with updates, add-ins, and more.

http://office.microsoft.com/ProductUpdates/

Microsoft Support Center
Valuable technical articles and resources on all Microsoft products, as well as access to a knowledge base with thousands of how-to and tech support articles on Outlook.

http://support.microsoft.com

Woody's Watch
Woody Leonhard's Advice, news, and newsletters on all Microsoft Office products, including Outlook.

http://www.woodyswatch.com

OutlookFAQ
A site with Outlook tips, techniques, and how-tos.

http://www.outlookfaq.com

Slipstick Systems
> A wonderful collection of resources on Microsoft Outlook and Microsoft Exchange Server for new users, experts, and administrators.
>
> *http://slipstick.com*

Outlook Newsgroups
> Microsoft maintains a news server that you can access using any newsreader. Most of the newsgroups on the server are also copied to other news servers, so you may already have access. All Outlook newsgroups start with *microsoft.public.outlook*, and there are groups on most Outlook topics.
>
> *msnews.microsoft.com*

Books

Outlook 2000 in a Nutshell. Tom Syroid and Bo Leuf. O'Reilly & Associates. A compact reference that uncovers all of Outlook's documented and undocumented features and shares powerful time-saving tips. Look for an updated version in 2003.

Microsoft Outlook Programming, Jumpstart for Administrators, Developers, and Power Users. Sue Mosher. Digital Press. Introduces Outlook programming and application development. When you're ready to go from power user to developer, this is the book to use.

Outlook Tools

ExLife
> A powerful alternative to Outlook's built-in Rules Wizard that lets you perform a dizzying number of actions on messages as they are received, sent, or created in any folder. It also works more reliably than the built-in Rules Wizard. You can have messages automatically processed

as they come in or when they are marked as read, or you can process them yourself with the click of a button. Free trial. Be sure to check out the differences between the standard and pro versions.

http://www.ornic.com

ExSign

An advanced signature manager that works with or without ExLife, supports multiple Exchange profiles, and lets you define different signature rules for each message type (new message, reply, forward, autoreply, and autoforward). Free trial.

http://www.ornic.com

SpamNet

A free spam-filtering tool that works inside Outlook and processes messages as they arrive. Simple to install and use, SpamNet sends suspected spam to a Spam folder for you to review later. A Block button sends any missed spam to the Spam folder and sends a message to Cloudmark so it can be added to their databases. An Unblock button lets you retrieve valid messages that were considered spam. Of the dozens of products I tried, this product is the most effective and the easiest to use. Plus, it's free.

http://cloudmark.com/products/spamnet/

Infuzer

This installs a small program in Windows that lets you easily copy scheduling information from the Web (on sites that use it) or an email message straight into your Outlook calendar. You can also create events and email them to other people who use Infuzer. Infuzer is free, but some premium services that use Infuzer (such as Weather.com) may charge a fee.

http://www.infuzer.com

Trust Filter

This Outlook add-in scans incoming emails and moves them to an Untrusted folder if the sender's email address is not on a special trust list that you set up. Simple controls let you add and remove people from your trusted list. Trust Filter is free.

http://www.benziegler.com/TrustFilter

Outlook Cleaner

This program (which is separate from Outlook) scans your Outlook items. A simple window shows all Outlook folders and the number of messages they contain. You can then delete hundreds or thousands of Outlook items across multiple folders by setting up simple criteria such as age, type of message, or subject.

http://www.personalcrm.com/Outlook_Cleaner.htm

DetachXP

This program works only with Outlook 2002. Use it to specify which types of attachments should be blocked. Free, but a donation is requested.

http://www.mcdev.com/outlook.shtml

TweakOL

This program works only with Outlook 2002. It adds four settings: always show the BCC field, minimize Outlook to the System Tray, disable MSN Messenger, and disable attachment security. Free, but a donation is requested.

http://www.mcdev.com/outlook.shtml

'Create New' Outlook Tools

These simple tools add fast access to common Outlook items (contacts, tasks, journal entries, email, and appointments) to the System Tray. You can double-click the tray icon to start a new item of that type, even when Outlook is not running. Free, but a donation is requested.

http://www.mcdev.com/outlook.shtml

Index

We'd like to hear your suggestions for improving our indexes. Send email to
index@oreilly.com.

Learn from experts.
Find the answers you need.

Sign up for a **10-day free trial** to get **unlimited access** to all of the content on Safari, including Learning Paths, interactive tutorials, and curated playlists that draw from thousands of ebooks and training videos on a wide range of topics, including data, design, DevOps, management, business—and much more.

Start your free trial at:
oreilly.com/safari

(No credit card required.)

Ingram Content Group UK Ltd.
Milton Keynes UK
UKHW020019100323
418330UK00009B/619